MODERN BRITISH BEER

WRITTEN AND
PHOTOGRAPHED BY

MATTHEW CURTIS

CAMRA
BOOKS

To Dad
For believing in me

Published by the Campaign for Real Ale Ltd.
230 Hatfield Road, St Albans, Hertfordshire AL1 4LW
United Kingdom

www.camra.org.uk/books

ISBN 978-1-85249-370-7

A CIP catalogue record for this book is available from the British Library

Printed and bound in the United Kingdom by Cambrian Printers Ltd,
Aberystwyth

Commissioning Editor: Katie Button, Alan Murphy
Copy Editor: Alan Murphy
Design/Typography: Dale Tomlinson
Cover Design: Tida Bradshaw
Sales & Marketing: Toby Langdon

Contents

contents cont...

ACKNOWLEDGEMENTS

Modern British Beer would have not come into being if it were not for the support of a great many wonderful people. Thanks firstly to Alan Murphy for believing in my idea, and for commissioning and editing the book, to Katie Button for seeing it through to completion, and Dale Tomlinson for page design and layout. Thanks to Toby Langdon, Alex Metcalfe and the amazing team at CAMRA helping make all this happen. Thank you to the many brewers who took the time to speak to me for this book. Special thanks to Mark Tranter at Burning Sky for agreeing to brew a beer to help launch the book.

Thanks to Tida Bradshaw for her amazing cover design, and to the many friends and peers who lent me their advice and support while I was working on the book: Jonny Hamilton, Lily Waite, Katie Mather, Nick Duke, Steph Shuttleworth, Claire Bullen, Doreen Joy Barber, Jonny Garrett, Paul Jones, Jimmy Hatherley, Kate and Adam Blaszczyk, Jen Ferguson and Glenn Williams, Melissa Cole, and Adrian Tierney-Jones. Apologies to anyone I forgot, but your support and friendship means a great deal to me all the same.

Special thanks to Pete Brown, for convincing me to 'wait for the right opportunity': I'm so glad I did. And to Chris Schooley at Troubadour Maltings in Colorado for helping me connect beer back to its agriculture. Thanks to my family, especially my dad, Frank, who started me on my beer journey. Lastly, and most importantly, thank you to my partner Dianne for your strength, guidance and love. I wouldn't have been able to do this without you.

Prologue

Over the past two decades, beer as we know it in Great Britain and Northern Ireland has changed: forever.

I'm aware this is something of a sweeping statement. A cry for attention, perhaps, as I begin to cobble together a hastily thought-out argument explaining why I think this is the case. The truth is, however, I have been thinking about this for a very long time. The subject of beer, and the endlessly fascinating culture that stems from it, is one I find so compelling it's typically the first thing to occupy my thoughts when I wake up, and is still rattling around my head at the end of the day.

Firstly, I think it's important to state, the fact that British beer has changed – or perhaps 'evolved' is the more appropriate term – is a very good thing. There has never been a better time to be a beer drinker on these islands. This is reflected in the proliferation of choice from thousands of breweries and hundreds of different styles; from the beautifully traditional to the tantalisingly ultra-modern. Many of these breweries are now also thinking more ethically, sustainably, agriculturally and deliciously in ways they weren't previously. All of which serves as a marker indicating how far we've come as a beer drinking, and beer loving, nation.

Throughout the pages of this book I'm going to attempt to put my thoughts into some kind of order and explain how I think beer in the United Kingdom has changed, and why I feel the evolution of British beer culture is so important to those of us who enjoy drinking it. To achieve this I'm going to present a series of short stories, each focusing on a particular beer and what makes it stand out; from how it tastes, to where its ingredients are sourced, to the people behind the scenes working hard to make it.

These beers will cover a wide range of different styles, from vibrantly hopped Pale Ales and IPAs to delectably dark Stouts and Porters, wild and funky Farmhouse Ales, rich and indulgent Red and Brown Ales and many more besides. The stories will also be broken down by region. Because, important as it is to highlight British beer as a whole, part of what makes this story so compelling is a noticeably increasing focus on provenance and a return to regionality – both in terms of flavour and personality. Every part of the country has its own story to tell, each adding its own traits to the personality of modern British beer.

As interesting and entertaining as they may be, these stories – presented individually – might not make a particularly compelling argument as to why I feel British beer has altered in such a huge way over the past twenty or so years. However, when they're woven together as a whole, everything begins to make a lot more sense. One thing about British beer culture that I hope we can agree on from the outset is that it's immensely complex, full of a rich and occasionally controversial history, with many quirks and facets that are regularly, and sometimes heatedly, debated. This is why I feel this book is so important as it aims to pull a common thread from all of those spirited discussions into something more concrete – a tangible idea we can all (mostly) agree upon.

Before we continue I feel it's also important to tell you what this book is not. This isn't a history book, nor is it a guide to beer that will explain to you where it is from and how it is made. And while I will include my own personal tasting notes when talking about each beer, these are designed to be evocative and thirst inducing. I'm not here to lecture you on what glass you should be

using, or how to employ your retronasal olfaction in order to best appreciate the elegant aroma of the beer in front of you. There are plenty of great books that do this already, and I don't feel the need to add to them.

Also, this is not some sort of manifesto; a my-way-or-the-high-way declaration that I demand you all agree with. Like the beer I recommend you pour yourself right now (go on, there's no time like the present), it's designed to be interpreted and enjoyed however you feel is best. This is a beer book that can be poured into your favourite glass or chugged straight from the can – I'm not fussy and neither should you be. What I hope you get from it is a reflection on how British beer has evolved, why this matters, what it means for our beer culture and to the ever-growing communities who enjoy drinking it.

This is a book about why modern British beer is important.

Beer, as a global cultural movement, is in a constant state of flux. An ever-shifting, seething mass of ideas, influences and history that, unlike a perfectly conditioned pint of real ale, never has a chance to properly settle. But just like a perfect pint, it is endlessly compelling.

Every generation has its own stories of beer, and therefore its own perception of what it is and where it fits into society. I know I've said this isn't a history book, but in terms of British beer it's hugely important to reflect (albeit briefly) on its past before focusing on the present; specifically the industrialisation and commoditization that has defined British beer for several centuries, and how a resistance to this defined what we drink today. Without its history there is no modern British beer.

Historically – and we're talking long before the days of empire and colonisation here – brewing beer in the United Kingdom was the role of women in the community. This is where the term 'brewster' originates from, specifically referring to women beer makers, and not men. It was the matriarchs within localised communities who brewed beer for sustenance and, in all likelihood, inebriation, for times of mirth and merriment just like we enjoy today.

It was we men who, in our infinite wisdom, decided that by making more beer we could make more money. The role of brewing – and therefore where it existed culturally – was eventually taken away from brewsters and smaller communities as production was vastly scaled up. Following the dawn of the Industrial Revolution in the 18th century, the idea of brewing as a capitalist venture became the norm. Britain's colonial era was also a huge factor in the expansion of beer as a commercial idea. Much of this, such as the shipping of strong, gratuitously hopped ale to countries such as India, has become somewhat over-romanticised as a result. The grim reality is that as the production of beer became industrialised, it was increasingly made for profit, not people.

One thing the history books do prove is that the colonial and industrial eras gave birth to early examples of what we refer to today as beer styles. As much as they might still be argued over (with some still claiming they don't really exist), it's this period from which beers like Stout, Porter, Mild and India Pale Ale (now almost universally abbreviated as IPA) would emerge. Eventually, the records of these historic recipes would be interpreted by modern brewers as they sought to create beers that are as delicious as they are compelling, marrying history with modern techniques and equipment.

The development of historic recipes and the beer styles that emerged from the industrialisation of brewing is hugely important to the story of modern British beer. Styles not only gave us a blueprint for how beers 'should' be made, but would eventually arm a new wave of innovators with rules to be broken. Modern beer exists at the nexus between what history has taught us about it, and those who would try to usurp these lessons. What unifies these ideas in terms of modern brewing is a return to the notion of community; brewing for the sustainment and enjoyment of those closest to you, just as the pre-industrial brewsters had done, long before the brewing of beer became more focused on financial gain than what was actually being brewed.

The onward march of the industrialisation of beer was disrupted in the 20th century due to the outbreak of the First and Second World Wars. Although hops and barley were still farmed and beer was still produced and consumed during these times, it was affected by rationing. This meant brewers were forced by law to alter their recipes. In the years that followed the Second World War, beer in the United Kingdom once again attempted to continue its expansion and commoditization. One response to this would set British beer culture on the path directly towards where it is now.

The formation of CAMRA (the Campaign for Real Ale) in 1971 was a glorious act of rebellion and defiance; one that beer as we know it today owes a debt of immense gratitude. At this time the 'Big Six' brewing corporations – Allied Breweries (Ansells, Ind Coope and Tetley), Bass, Courage, Grand Metropolitan (Watney Mann & Truman), Scottish & Newcastle and Whitbread – accounted for 75% of beer production in the UK. They also owned and controlled the majority of retail outlets, which back then meant pubs.

CAMRA's passion for the conservation of real ale was much more than an attempt to save a method of dispense that was declining in popularity. It was about preserving the idea that beer is delicious, and serves as an anchor for the communities that gather in the places where it is served. Despite the Campaign's efforts, in 2021 some 72% of beer production in the UK is still owned by just five breweries – Anheuser-Busch InBev, Heineken, Molson Coors, Carlsberg and Asahi – none of whom are headquartered in the United Kingdom.

However – and this part is crucial – while there were just 170 breweries in the UK in 1971, it is now home to almost 2,300, most of which are small, independent and focused on serving their local communities with a delicious variety of beer. Each one with its own history, no matter how brief, and its own interpretations of how beer should be made. There are many factors to this boom, from the financial to the political and socio-economic, but the main reason is people. Throughout the last fifty years – perhaps most significantly since the turn of the century – people became more interested in drinking an increasingly interesting and flavourful variety of beers than ever before. Much of which is proof, for me at least, of how

significant CAMRA's influence has been, and continues to be, on the public's desire to enjoy great beer.

Perhaps one of the largest unforeseen impacts CAMRA had on the preservation of real ale and the modernisation of British beer was not in the UK but in the United States. From the late 1970s to the present day, the burgeoning North American beer scene took great influence from the historical beer culture of European countries like Belgium, Germany, the Czech Republic, and our own real ale culture here in Britain. When this influence was catalysed by the American's inherent entrepreneurial spirit, it created an explosion. Since then, the US has spent the past few decades redefining its beer legacy from that of light Lager to one of the most vibrant and eclectic beer cultures anywhere in the world. Much of this attitude originates from when American brewers eagerly began recreating the characterful cask beers they tasted on visits to the UK: beers that may not have existed if CAMRA hadn't stepped in to slow the march of the UK's biggest breweries.

We've come to refer to this changing dynamic that began in North America as the 'Craft Beer Revolution'. It's impossible to ignore the 9,000 breweries that exist today in the US, and the fact that over 20,000 exist globally, many of which look, act, and think as closely to their American counterparts as possible. North America also produces over 40% of the world's annual hop harvest – one of beer's four key ingredients along with water, yeast and malted grain. The US presently grows more hops than any other country in the world, but only within the last decade, as demand for its potent, aromatic varieties eventually squeezed Germany into second place. By comparison, England cultivates just 2% of the world's hops. Over the past forty years the US has grown to become the largest and most powerful brewing nation in the world. Where they go, the rest of the modern brewing world follows.

Despite the massive influence modern American beer culture has had on British brewing over the past twenty years, modern British beer is not merely a pastiche of it, though such is the breadth of the US beer industry's influence it can often feel this way. But while some breweries in the UK draw more influence from the US than others, almost as many will do so from Germany, or New Zealand, or solely from the deep lexicon of British brewing history. All of which feeds into the cultural melting pot I refer to as modern British beer.

*

Important though the history of British beer and what has shaped its culture may be, it's also crucial to recognise that everyone views its evolution and transformation through their own lens. Mine was initially through the eyes of my father, Frank. A child of the early 1950s, he began his journey into beer culture in the 1970s as a student in Sheffield. I still love hearing his stories from when he worked in a local pub called The Beehive. In fact, it was stories like these, and the beers he would share with me (when I was old enough) that subconsciously nudged me along the path towards a career writing about it.

A pretty typical pub of the time, popular with students and working-class men alike, The Beehive stood out. Instead of the near-ubiquitous local Stones Bitter, it served Tetley's, which was brewed in Leeds. This is significant, not just because of how fiercely territorial people were about their local brands at the time, but because in Sheffield Tetley's was more expensive. Loyal fans would happily travel to The Beehive to drink it, and pay more for the privilege. Behavior that, to me, feels very similar to the beer enthusiasts of today, who travel far and wide to try their favourite beers with little regard for the expense.

When my dad worked there, from 1977–78, the Tetley's was served from 54-gallon 'hogsheads' – heavy wooden barrels holding a massive 432 pints each, which could easily create enough force to

send someone to an early grave if not handled with great care when rolled into the cellar. At busy times the pub would have four of these monsters ready to go, as the denizens of the Steel City sought to quench their great thirst after a hard day's graft.

'Eight pints of bitter, and a half for tha' self,' would be the order. At least that's how Dad tells it. Throughout service it would be repeated over and over again until last orders were called. There was no request for samples, or customers diligently working their way across the pumps as they tasted through a varied selection of local beers. This was a session beer in the purest sense of the word.

I often reflect on these memories as a reminder of how much things have changed over the past fifty years, and how wildly different my experience of beer was when I came of age, right at the turn of the century. I am a Millennial in the truest sense of the word, and (at first reluctantly) I have come to wear that label with dignity.

By the time I reached my early twenties, mass-market European Lagers were dominant, and hostelries that offered an interesting and varied range of real ales were incredibly intimidating to us young drinkers seeking a buzz. Not just because of their shady interiors and much older clientele, but because to enter one was to lose all credibility among your peers. In the early 2000s beer in the United Kingdom – specifically real ale – was not even close to the idea of being cool. The unfortunate and often misplaced stereotype of the beard-wearing, socks- and sandals-clad beer enthusiast was stuck fast to the face of British beer like an old, crusty scab. It would take the aforementioned influence of the United States to eventually prise it from its fixtures.

As fate would have it, in 2010 my dad – who had long since introduced me to the wonders of cask-conditioned real ale (as well as a wide variety of gleefully intoxicating Belgian beers) – emigrated to the US. On my first visit to his new home in Fort Collins, Colorado, I discovered the life-changing, vibrantly delicious, Pale and Amber Ales, Stouts, Porters – and whatever else I could get my hands on – that would instantly transform me into the beer fanatic I am today.

In fact, I can pinpoint the exact moment beer ceased to be something I merely enjoyed drinking, and became what I would spend almost every waking hour obsessing over. It was in the taproom at Odell Brewing, just after lunchtime on 1 July 2010, on my first taste of their eponymous IPA: a moment that could be described as viewing something in high-definition technicolour for the first time after previously experiencing it only in fuzzy black and white. I tasted fresh orange peel and citrus zest in great waves, each one underpinned by the rich, biscuit-like fixture of malted barley, both culminating in a riotously bitter finish that hoisted me by the lapels and demanded I take another sip. It is perhaps a small irony that I would later find out the brewery's co-founder, Doug Odell, was inspired to start brewing after a trip to Britain, and tasting its fine ales.

When I returned home from that visit, everything had changed. I was intent on finding out more about every brewery I could, with my thinking being that if I could find breweries making beers this wonderfully delicious and exciting in the US, then I would also be able to find them in the UK. This led me to discover what was, at the time, a smaller, less established, yet no less compelling modern beer scene. And it was slowly beginning to proliferate beyond the fringes of geekdom, where it predominantly existed, gradually creeping into the consciousness of the mainstream. New breweries were beginning to emerge at an exponential rate, many inspired by the excitement in America. Between 2010 and 2020 the number of active breweries in the UK more than doubled. My reaction to this was to start a beer blog.

Near the beginning of this new brewery boom in the UK, one particular Scottish enterprise would emerge to alter the course of contemporary British brewing history like no other. Regardless of how you feel about BrewDog – and for me this can often shift within a period of minutes – it's impossible to deny that their rapid rise to prominence was a game-changer for British beer. Founded in 2007 by James Watt and Martin Dickie in the town of Fraserburgh, in the north-east of Scotland, the duo (who were then only in their mid-twenties) injected beer culture in the United Kingdom with an – arguably much-needed – 'fuck you' attitude, sticking two fingers up at tradition in an attempt to forcibly drag it into the 21st century. At times this backfired on them, as such an attitude inevitably will, but that does little to diminish the mark they made.

It would be arrogant, however, to lay such plaudits at the feet of a single brewery. As game changing as the Scottish brewery's arrival was, theirs was just one in a series of catalysts that caused the face of British beer to permanently alter. A couple of years before BrewDog there was the arrival of Thornbridge, in Bakewell, Derbyshire, where eventual BrewDog co-founder Martin Dickie cut his brewing teeth. In 1997, way before either of the aforementioned breweries were even a pipe dream, Marble Brewery began producing increasingly bitter and aromatic beers at the back of the Marble Arch pub on Rochdale Road, near the centre of Manchester. And before then there was Dark Star Brewery, in the cellars of the Evening Star, Brighton, which was established in 1994.

The shift we've seen in the ethos of British brewers, away from the industrialised, mass production of the past, towards an increasing focus on small-batch, artisanal brewing, happened long before the arrival of this century's modern breweries. It would be remiss of me not to mention Brendan Dobbin, founder of the (long since closed) West Coast Brewing Company in Manchester, or Sean Franklin, the original founder of Rooster's Brewing in Harrogate, North Yorkshire. They were two of the first brewers to use modern, North American hop varieties in the UK, slowly but surely ushering in a new ideology within British brewing; one that would take decades before it was fully realised and understood, not just by their fellow brewers but by us drinkers. As exciting as the past two decades have been for beer in the UK, the efforts and influence of those who came before cannot be celebrated loudly enough.

But I was too young to experience this when it happened. Like I said, everyone's experience of beer occurs exclusively through

their own lens. Speaking as a (now former) Londoner of fifteen years, one of the biggest shifts in the course of British brewing that I did witness was the arrival of The Kernel brewery in 2009. Where BrewDog was loud and brash, here was a brewery that was graceful and modest. I will never forget the first time my curiosity was piqued when I came across their bottles clad in their plain brown labels, only to discover their contents were anything but plain.

Despite how completely different their image and ethos appeared externally, The Kernel and BrewDog were aligned in the way that their beers possessed both depth and vibrancy. Both were channelling a huge amount of US influence, but were also gradually twisting it into something else; honing it, making it their own. Their emergence would, quite literally, inspire thousands of new British breweries. Some would pursue a similar path in the name of flavour and deliciousness, while others would look to the old ways of the industrial-era brewers, desiring constant expansion and growth. Some, including BrewDog itself, would attempt to align the two, as a new era of British brewing history began to write its own story.

What was curious about beer in the early 2000s, however, is that much of the new wave was choosing to cast aside the somewhat tired image of traditional British real ale culture; the very same one that felt like such a barrier to me in my earliest beer drinking days. This desire to overwrite the past was something I was in support of at the time, but now I feel was a huge mistake. Eschewing the oldest of our country's brewing traditions only serves to reduce its legacy. There is plenty within Britain's chequered past that does deserve to be consigned to the dustbin of history, but our greatest beer tradition – that of real ale, served from cask via gravity or beer engine – is not one of them.

Modern British Beer is not a celebration of modernity alone. Without its rich past, from historic recipes to the deeply important ritual and culture of cask ale, it would not exist at all. British real ale culture deserves to be celebrated and cherished in the same way people revere Helles in Bavaria, Pilsner in the Czech Republic and IPA along the Californian West Coast. As important as carving its own path has been, it is only when British beer culture fully embraces its history that it can truly become modern.

That we each view beer through our own lens and make it our own experience is important. And equally important is that we remind ourselves that, although British beer has indeed changed significantly, none of the positives have been taken away, only added to. You can, and should still, enjoy your perfectly conditioned pint of cask bitter as much as you should your Lager, Pale Ale, nitrogenated Stout or wild-fermented, barrel-aged farmhouse Saison.

Modern British beer exists on what I have recently begun to refer to as 'The Broad Spectrum of Joy'. The spectrum is not linear – consider it more of a flat circle, one that takes in every single element of British beer, from the furthest reaches of its past to the cutting edge of its present. On one part of the spectrum there might be someone enjoying a sweet Stout infused with lactose, cacao and vanilla, while at another they might be enjoying a Golden Ale that celebrates nothing but the finest barley and hops. Indeed all beer, and the culture that stems from it, exists on the same spectrum. You can pull joy from any part of it you want, at any time. No one at another part is able to take away from your own experience.

This all boils down to the idea that we drink beer because it is a joyful act, and when it comes to the idea of beer in a modern sense nothing could be truer. Whether it's a can or two at home, a bottle generously shared with friends, a quick pint at the local on the way home, or a night of revelry with your finest friends, we drink beer because it makes us laugh and smile.

Wherever each of us might reside on the Broad Spectrum of Joy at any particular time, it is important that we admit to ourselves that British beer has changed forever, and that this is a wonderful thing. Imagine coming of drinking age now in 2021 and having to select your first legally purchased beer from a choice of literally thousands of breweries, some of which have made hundreds of different beers. Imagine all of the joyful experiences that person will have as they begin a beer journey of their own. That great beer can be such a pivotal experience in our lives is what makes it truly magnificent.

DEFINING MODERN BRITISH BEER

Before we dig into the stories behind some of the most fascinating beers that make up the rich tapestry of modern beer culture in the United Kingdom, I feel we should set a few ground rules. We've reflected on the idea of modern British beer in a historical and philosophical sense. And we've established the fact that the primary function of modern beer is to spark joy. Based on my experiences with beer over the past decade I feel it's essential that we now give modern British beer a proper definition; without it, the rest of this book will fall apart before it even gets going.

You'll notice the relative absence of the term 'craft beer' in this book. I actually like the term craft beer a lot, and use it regularly in other writing. The word 'craft' in itself is the perfect way to describe the merging of the more artisanal and creative elements of brewing with those rooted in the disciplines of science and engineering. For me, it is the perfect balance of these skills that makes up the archetypal modern brewer.

So heated has the debate been over the meaning of craft beer, and to where and what it should be applied, I have decided to largely sidestep its use in this book. For example, there are still those who believe that the term 'craft beer' does not apply to real ale. The dissonance that this reductive argument creates runs against my theory that modern beer exists on the Broad Spectrum of Joy, which, as we've established, is the idea that all beer is there to be enjoyed, regardless of its place within beer culture.

To avoid the same thing happening to the term 'modern beer' I've decided to define it using five specific points. During the process of researching this book and speaking to each brewery about their featured beer, I also took the opportunity to ask them exactly what 'modern British beer' meant to them. As I expected, few were able to give me the same answer, which incentivised me to ensure my definition was solid.

'I guess for me modern British beer is beer made by breweries with intent, purpose and honesty, and trying to make fantastic products,' Theo Freyne of Cheltenham's Deya Brewing Company tells me, while admitting in the following sentence that American brewing's influence on British beer over the past decade has been 'palpable'.

'It can feel like a totally male, generational war at times, beards of the 70s battling it out with beards of the 2020s for whose product is superior,' came the response from Jan Rogers, who has run Marble Brewery in Manchester since it was founded in 1997. '[I] find it totally amazing that industry people with such good sense have got caught up in an "America's best" mythology.'

'Perhaps we should be taking more influence from our own brewing traditions closer to home,' Theo from Deya adds. 'In the last few years, breweries making excellent examples of more classic styles have really excited me.'

Despite the wide range of responses I received, the more I asked the question common threads began to emerge, slowly but surely. When I combined these with my own ideas, I was able to construct what I felt best defined modernity within British beer culture. At present, not all of the following five points apply to every single brewery that's featured in this book. But the majority of them do, which for me is a unifier, reinforcing my argument that today's British beer culture is not a scattered mess of conflicting ideas, but exists as a 'scene' in the truest sense of the world.

Before we proceed, I feel it's important to point out that you may notice the absence of certain beers or breweries which have played an important role in the development of modern British beer culture over the past decade or so. This is because I have decided to concentrate on breweries that are (at the time of this book going to print) still independently owned and run. If I cannot consider a brewery's parent company to be modern, then neither is the brewery in question. As a bonus, this freed up valuable space to tell you about a few wonderful small breweries that you may not have heard of before.

Another reason some breweries are missing from this book is that there simply wasn't enough room. I didn't want this to merely be a list of beers for you to tick off. This is a collection of stories that hopefully bring as much joy when you read them as you would receive when drinking the beers themselves. Whittling down the selection was the most challenging part of putting this book together. I hope you'll forgive me if a beer or brewery you're incredibly fond of didn't make the cut.

Finally, it's also worth pointing out that this definition, and in fact the entirety of this book, is more of a thesis than anything else. This is not a stone tablet I've carried down from a scared mountain top. Please take everything you read within these pages with a healthy pinch of salt. One thing I do hope we can all agree on, however, is that if drinking beer is a joyful act, then adhering to these five points is a way of ensuring that joy doesn't simply exist as a fleeting moment, but is nurtured for beer drinkers both now, and in the future.

Modern British Beer: A Definition

Modern British Beer is focused on ingredients, their agriculture and provenance

A point that's often lost amid the jungle of discourse is that beer is something that is grown in the ground. If I were writing a book about cider making, you would immediately be able to connect that to the orchard, and with wine, the vineyard. But when you imagine the production of beer, you're more likely to think about processes such as mashing grain, of steaming kettles and rows of stainless steel vessels. Not verdant strings of hop bines, or golden rows of barley. A better way to think of beer in a modern sense, and to inspire a deeper connection between it and the drinker, is to link it directly back to its agriculture.

This does exist loosely in the way we talk about individual hop varieties like Mosaic, Saaz or East Kent Goldings, and with barley varieties such as Maris Otter, Genie, and Golden Promise. But when beer drinkers consider these ingredients it's not in the same way as they might do a Pinot Noir, or Tremblett's Bitter (one of the finest names for a cider apple variety I've ever come across). By establishing a stronger connection to the provenance of beer's ingredients, it creates a story that can only serve to enhance the feeling of delight you experience when you take that first sip of a freshly poured pint.

Modern breweries care about the provenance of their ingredients, from their hops and barley to water and yeast, and anything else they feel so inclined to add to their beer. In an ideal situation a brewer should be able to tell you the name of the farm, or even better, the farmer, who grew them. Modern breweries should be completely transparent about their supply chains, be interested in experimenting with both new and heritage varieties of hops and grain alike, and dedicated to properly supporting the agricultural systems that sustain their breweries while doing so.

Some of my very best experiences in beer have been treading through towering hop bines, or watching a maltster as they work hard to convert harvested barley into malt so that it can be used in the making of beer. For me these moments have been as poignant as mucking in on a brew day, or heading to a favourite pub for a pint or two. Deepening the connection between drinkers and beer's agriculture will only enhance their understanding and experience of it.

Modern British Beer is invested in sustainability, and the preservation of the environment

As much as it benefits the modern brewery to be invested in the provenance of their ingredients, so too does it to be mindful of their impact on the environment. As much as it pains me to say it, brewing, and the systems linked to it, are not sustainable practices. It is largely reliant on industrialised agriculture for its ingredients. It generates a huge amount of wastewater (for every pint brewed, another five pints of water are required for its manufacture). It puts pressures on the supply chain with its huge demand for glass and aluminium for packaging. It needs pressurised carbon dioxide for both production and dispense. Beer is perishable, and so uses a vast amount of refrigeration to stay fresh for longer, adding to the energy its production sucks up. Not to mention the rigorous cleaning a brewery requires, which depends on chemicals including peracetic acid and sodium hydroxide (the latter more commonly referred to by brewers as caustic).

Globally, brewing is largely the preserve of a handful of multinationals that control the majority of its resources and supply chain. This means that smaller breweries have a far less significant impact on the environment than their larger counterparts, but for many of them that impact is still negative. In order for future generations to enjoy beer as we do, modern breweries must seek to be as environmentally sustainable as possible, reducing their impact on our planet wherever they can. It is the moral duty of the modern British brewery to take on this responsibility.

The good news is that this is happening, albeit slowly. In Scotland, BrewDog – the largest brewery to feature in this book by some distance – has an output that is officially 'carbon negative' and has recently seen it certified as a B Corporation. This is only awarded to 'businesses that meet the highest standards of verified social and environmental performance, public transparency, and legal accountability to balance profit and purpose,' according to B Lab, the non-profit organisation which manages the certification. Other notable B Corps include ethical shoemaker Allbirds and outdoor fashion brand Patagonia.

This book features several examples of breweries whose efforts to support the environment match those to create the best beers possible. These include Stroud Brewery in Gloucestershire, which is dedicated to using organically produced ingredients, Good Things in East Sussex, which has invested heavily in sustainable energy, and Purity Ales in Warwickshire, which has created its own reed bed system for the safe return of its wastewater to the local environment. A dedication to greater sustainability, and consideration of the long term impact of the production of beer on the environment, is an essential facet of the modern British brewery.

Purity Brewing Co have created a reed bed filtration system to safely return wastewater to the environment.

Modern British Beer is focused on regionality and is driven by, and supportive of, its local communities

The recent effect of external influences on British brewing, in particular the American Craft Beer Revolution, have had an inversely proportional effect on the regional diversity of British beer. A significant number of newer British breweries demonstrated a strong intention to ape their counterparts in the United States. This resulted in the creation of increasingly hyperbolic beers, some almost single-mindedly focused on the sheer volume of hops that could be crammed into a single batch. But many of these recipes were, in fact, highly alike, using the same hops in similar recipes to create beers that look, taste, and smell the same as everyone else. This ran against the idea that 'craft beer' is a space for innovators. The result of this copycat behavior established the idea – particularly in those outside of beer's most niche circles – that modern beer is homogenous, and that the pursuit of uniformity was its ultimate goal.

Admittedly, a fair amount of wonderful beer has emerged from this way of thinking, but so did an endless plethora of near identical, hazy, mid-strength Pale Ales; a complete lack of original ideas creating blandness out of excitement. What makes modern British beer stand out is its depth in terms of the styles, flavours and experiences it can reward drinkers with. As dominant as the Pale Ale and IPA categories are, modern British beer is not merely a representation of these styles alone. This is a place for Bitters and Milds, Saisons and Amber Ales, Lagers, Porters and more besides. For beer to be truly modern there should be no boundaries, creating limitless possibilities for deliciousness.

Despite the encroachment of 5% Hazy Pale Ales brewed with Citra and Mosaic hops, I believe we are witnessing the gradual emergence of a different trend. For example, an IPA brewed under a railway arch in Bermondsey, South London, does not taste the same as one brewed in a warehouse in Manchester, on a farm

in Norfolk, or on an industrial estate in Cheltenham, and so on.
As we've already learned, the number of breweries in the UK
has exploded over the past decade. The result of this saturation
is that many of these breweries are learning that what sets them
apart is as important as the common ties that bind them together.

As a result we're seeing a trend of more breweries investing
their time, not just in creating beers that are unique to themselves
but that also celebrate regional provenance as a point of difference.
A knock-on effect being that as more modern breweries invest in
their inherent regionality, the more likely their local communities
will identify with them, and the investment of their time and
money in the support of that business will feel worthwhile.
Although regionality like this has been a hallmark of British
beer for decades (think back my anecdote about Stone's Bitter
and Tetley's in Sheffield), and it may feel like craft beer tried to
stamp it out through homogeneity, this couldn't be further from
the truth. Regionality is alive and well in modern British beer.

*The Kernel Brewery,
under the arches at
Spa Terminus, London*

Have multinational breweries and large retailers attempted to stamp out these cultural variances in the name of profit? Absolutely! Sameness is safe, and it sells. But increasingly, people are looking for more stimulation from the food and drink they consume, and are becoming increasingly mindful about where they choose to spend their money. This includes beer. So while part of what makes modern British beer so wonderful is the increasing diversity among breweries and what they offer, so too is the increasing diversity of the communities they support. The intrinsic link between the two is what makes it stand out from the mass-produced products that line the supermarket shelves.

Modern British Beer is inclusive and equitability-minded

While on the subject of community and diversity – as blindingly obvious as this should be to most of you reading this – I feel it's important to state that beer culture as a whole is still dominated by white, straight men. And as a white man who identifies as being straight, I admit that I am part of this distinct lack of diversity. For British beer to truly be considered modern, this must change.

This dynamic has been slowly shifting in more recent times, but not nearly fast enough. The reason things are changing is thanks to an increase in voices from marginalised communities (by which I mean anyone who is not a straight, white man) within beer, and a gradual trend of those who hold the power in beer stepping aside and allowing these voices to be heard. British beer culture is increasingly home to women, Black, Asian and other ethnic minorities, as well as the many different LGTBQ+ communities – people who love beer just as much as you or I do.

That this is happening is thanks to the immense efforts of folks like beer writer Melissa Cole, writer and activist Lily Waite and The Queer Brewing Project, activists such as Dr J. Nichol Jackson-Beckham, publications like Burum Collective, organisations such as Beer Kulture and Crowns & Hops in the USA, and many, many

other incredible, influential people. As their voices grow louder, so too does beer become a more welcoming space. But this can only happen effectively if people who already have the privilege of existing in beer communities can uncouple themselves from them, and boost the signal of the folks who are cultivating change.

Modern breweries are willing to take on this responsibility, and work through the challenges that making beer a truly equitable space presents every single day. It can be a difficult truth to swallow that beer culture is not inclusive, and that it remains an incredibly intimidating space to those outside of it. In order to be truly modern beer must not only be welcoming to all, but actively against the hatred that exists both inside and outside of it. Racism, sexism, transphobia, homophobia and all other forms of marginalising language and actions belong in the dustbin of beer's past, not its present, and certainly not its future.

Lily Waite works to highlight the lack of LGTBQ+ representation in today's beer culture.

Modern British Beer is delicious

This is perhaps the most obvious part of my definition, but one that still needs repeating. Drinking beer is an act of joy. Therefore, to spark that warm, fuzzy feeling from your first sip to your last, the beer you have in your hand must, first and foremost, also be delicious. If you are running a brewery that is ethical, equitable, community-minded, focused on sustainability, transparent with regards to its supply chain, and dedicated towards supporting those at either end of it, from the farmer to the drinker, but your beer still sucks, it is not modern British beer. Beer should be delicious, all of the time, and we could do with reminding ourselves of that simple truth once in a while.

Now that we've established our definition we can finally sink our teeth into the most important part of the book, the very essence of modern British beer, the beers themselves. Before we do though, I think it's worth pointing out that this definition is still freshly cast, and malleable. It's something I look forward to discussing with you all over the coming months and years. This is also an excellent time for you to top up that glass, because the following chapters will likely make you very, very thirsty.

A quick note on styles: Over the following chapters I've decided to list each beer by location, alcohol by volume (ABV) and style. The latter is loosely based on beer styles as defined by the Beer Judge Certification Program (BJCP), although I have tweaked this slightly to bring it up to date, and to distinguish between variants within a similar style, such as IPA. The idea of this is that it hopefully helps you understand a little more about the beer if you haven't tried it before. I've made sure to select beers that are also produced at least once per year. Hopefully, you should be able to get hold of them easily enough when they're available.

SCOTLAND

Black Isle

BrewDog

ABERDEEN
Fierce Beer

Six°North

Fyne Ales

Harviestoun

GLASGOW
Overtone

EDINBURGH
Newbarns
Pilot
Vault City

Tempest

There's no better place to start digging into the beers that define modern British beer as we know it than in Scotland.

Thinking back to the definition we established in the previous chapter – particularly to what I see as a renewed focus on regionality – part of me thinks it would've almost been wiser to release a series of books called *Modern English Beer*, *Modern Scottish Beer*, *Modern Welsh Beer* and so on. This is the reason why this book is broken down by location, as opposed to beer style, or chronologically.

Where I've decided to draw my boundaries will no doubt be a source of some scrutiny, but I believe this debate is part of the intrinsic nature of modern British beer and why it's so special. For such a small group of islands, British and Northern Irish people are remarkably tribal in their enthusiasm for beer. You could perhaps use another foodstuff, the bread roll, by way of comparison. Do you call it a bap? A cob? A barm cake? Whatever your name for it, you're probably incredibly defensive of that term. Beer is much the same in that where it has a specific regionality, people are inherently protective of it. Although 'passion' would perhaps be a better way to describe it, rather than defensiveness.

But why begin with stories from north of the border? Well, for better or worse, in terms of modern British beer, no brewery has had more significant an impact on brewing in the United Kingdom over the past twenty years than BrewDog. Love them or hate them, this is a hill I have chosen to die on. The sheer tenacity shown by founders James Watt and Martin Dickie in dragging the UK beer scene into the present by aping US counterparts such as

Stone Brewing, Dogfish Head and Sierra Nevada was astounding. It could not have been predicted when they founded their brewery in 2007 and released a beer called Punk IPA that it would one day become the best-selling independently brewed beer in the country, let alone that their brewery would become an internationally recognised brand, with production facilities on four continents. Their influence cannot be overstated.

But the impact of Scottish beer on British beer culture as a whole stretches way beyond the efforts of Watt, Dickie and the empire they've created. To give them so much credit would do the rest of this wonderful brewing nation a huge disservice. At roughly 120 operating breweries (at the time of this book going to print), Scotland actually has relatively few compared to other regions in the UK: London alone has more, as do Yorkshire and Greater Manchester. Another notable difference between Scotland and the rest of the country is that, outside of its large cities like Glasgow, Edinburgh, Aberdeen and Dundee, local pub culture doesn't quite look the same as it does south of the border. Head to the Highlands or Islands, for example, and you'll find licensed premises don't have the means or intention to sell real ale. This means that Scotland has fewer outlets for cask ale, a fast turnover product vital for the survival of many small breweries.

This means that modern beer in Scotland has had to find alternative ways to develop. Compared to their English counterparts, Scottish brewers have had to shout louder and work harder to get their voices heard. The sheer level of gumption possessed by this wonderful nation's breweries is testament to this. Once again you could use BrewDog as an example here, but you could also look towards the irreverent attitude of Pilot, the tenacity of Black Isle, or the appropriately named Fierce Beer. The end result of this inherent resourcefulness is an incredibly high standard of beer for a country possessing so few breweries relative to the size of its landmass.

Perhaps what's most remarkable about modern Scottish beer is its diversity in terms of the sheer breadth of styles and flavours it offers. Traditional Scottish beers, such as the 'shilling' denoted pub ales of the past (one of the last survivors being McEwan's 80/-, often nicknamed 'heavy' by locals), or classics such as Traquair House Ale, all have one thing in common: they are brown and taste predominantly of malted barley, and not much else. There is nothing wrong with this, and many of these beers are delicious, but they don't quite fit my idea of modernity.

From the 1990s onwards, the emergence of the Blonde Ale from Scotland's slowly growing wave of new breweries was something of a game changer. This was also an act of rebellion, which, as we've already learned, is something that has always defined a shift in brewing culture. These pale and (for the time) riotously hoppy beers gave eager Scottish drinkers something new to get their teeth into; beers like Black Isle Blonde and Fyne Ales Jarl. In fact, Jarl was allegedly the second *ever* beer in the UK to be brewed with North American Citra hops. Practically unheard of in 2009, it's now the most cultivated variety in the world. If that's not a signifier of modern Scottish beer, well, I don't know what is.

Something I also find amusing is that Scottish brewers and drinkers resolutely refuse to refer to these beers using English terms such as 'Bitter' or 'Golden Ale', despite them being very much of their ilk. They have well and truly made these styles their own. But despite the thoroughly deserved lack of love for the English, there are plenty of international influences that modern Scottish breweries were happy to adopt. Take Six°North channelling their love for Belgium into the beers they artfully create, or Overtone Brewing in Glasgow, who focus American influence into ultra-modern styles such as New England IPA and heavily Fruited Sour beers.

Beer in Scotland is almost like its own microcosm; a close-up view through the lens of modern beer culture in the UK as a whole. It possesses a willingness to absorb as much information about beer making from all over the world, but then transforms it into something that is resolutely and definitively Scottish. Without Scotland's influence, beer in the UK today would look very different indeed.

Slàinte mhath.

Fyne Ales
Jarl

Location: Cairndow, Argyll
Style: Blonde Ale | *ABV:* 3.8%

There are few greater beer experiences to be had in Scotland than to sit among the blue, green and grey folds of Glen Fyne, a plate of freshly shucked Loch Fyne oysters in one hand and a pint of Fyne Ale's iconic Golden Ale (or Blonde, if you prefer), Jarl, in the other.

On taking a glass of this remarkable, yet elegant beer to your lips you will at once feel regal, powerful and content. It's no coincidence this beer's name refers to the Norse *Jarls* or 'chiefs' of old. Jarl rasps at your palate, its sweetness dialled down to a whisper, leaving nowhere for its bold flavours of pithy grapefruit and lemon to hide.

But as sharply as these flavours descend, so too do they depart. This beer's vivacity is matched by a dry, bitter finish, and an effortlessly drinkable character, which, at only 3.8%, can, on occasion, seem to rapidly evaporate from your glass between sips. Due to its strength, it's arguably best suited to cask dispense – the gentle carbonation lending Jarl a little more body. However, if you do take my advice and pair it with some local oysters, the boost of effervescence provided by the keg version will enhance both the sweetness and salinity of every bite. Such is its quality, Jarl is a beer that works beautifully, regardless of how it's served.

'Beers like Jarl are meant to be in the middle of the table bringing people together and facilitating great times and good memories,' Fyne Ales' Jamie Delap tells me. 'We hope that it will bring a connection to the farm and glen where we brew and the team that brews it. Possibly embodied by a visit they have made to us, or wherever they have come across our beers.'

Glen Fyne is home to the 4,500 acre family farm on which founder, Tuggy Delap, and her sons, Jamie and Mungo, run their brewery. Established by Tuggy and husband, Jonny, in 2001, Fyne Ales brewed its first ever beer – the aptly named Highlander – on 30 November that year, which by no coincidence is also St Andrew's Day. After a period of ill health, Jonny passed away in 2009, after which Jamie assumed the role of managing director.

A few years prior to Jonny's passing, Fyne Ales recruited Wil Wood as head brewer. An industry veteran, Wil is perhaps better known for his more recent tenure at Lacons Brewery in Norfolk. In 2007 he would develop a beer called Avalanche using the North American Cascade and Liberty hop varieties. This bright, bitter beer, packed with aromatic citrus character, was an exciting sign of things to come. Three years later Wil would create another US-hopped beer. Only this time he'd got wind of a new, particularly remarkable variety known as Citra, which his former colleague, John Bryan, at Oakham Brewery in Peterborough had used to create an eponymously named beer – the first in the UK to do so.

The beer was launched as a special in June 2010 at the first ever FyneFest, a now annual gathering held each summer in Glen Fyne. On its debut the festival attracted only 150 attendees, whereas now they welcome over 3,000 guests to their estate every year. Jarl was an instant hit, and over the course of its life would forever change the fortunes and direction of Fyne Ales.

'Jarl has become the central expression of our brewing identity,' Jamie tells me. 'When in 2014 we were ready to make a major investment in a new brewery, we designed it explicitly to brew the best versions of Jarl that we possibly could. It enabled us to lift Jarl up to another level, while also giving us the platform to build out from with other styles and presentations of beer.'

FyneFest

For me there are few better expressions of both modern Scottish and British beer than Jarl. It encapsulates the righteous traditions of our drinking culture – a low ABV, sessionable beer, that's also affordable to most people – but with a choice of ingredients that was, and still is, resolutely cutting edge. That it is also imbued with such a strong sense of place and purpose, arguably makes it one of the most important beers being brewed in the UK today. It's a beer that should be drunk whenever you see it. But – and take this from me – it always seems to taste better when enjoyed in the glen.

BrewDog
Punk IPA

Location: **Ellon, Aberdeenshire**
Style: **American IPA** | *ABV:* **5.4%**

Do you remember your first Punk IPA?

While the memory of my own might have become a little rose-tinted over time, it remains no less poignant. I recall striding up to the bar at The Dove in Hammersmith, West London, and spotting the now infamous blue-shield featuring a curved, barking dog (designed to not-so-subtly mimic the Saltire flag of Scotland.) It was late 2010, and having only recently experienced my own American beer epiphany, the sight of this beer on draught sent a tingle down my spine. This was one of the most exciting new breweries in the country and I was finally about to taste its beer on draught.

Sitting down with our freshly poured pints, a friend and I watched patiently as the last few off-white bubbles settled at the rim of the glass before simultaneously taking deep sips. Smiling back at me, my companion set his glass back on the table and announced, 'this tastes just like Sierra Nevada Pale Ale!' Recounting the American classic that inspired a generation of brewers, before immediately returning the glass to his lips for another taste.

Two things in particular stand out from this memory: firstly, that my pint was served from a cask, and that it was the only time I would actually experience Punk in this format (BrewDog ceased production of cask ale in July 2011); and secondly, that, at the time, I had absolutely zero clue as to what kind of behemoth this beer

would grow into. The way Punk brashly chanelled its American influences in its own image would forever alter the perception of what British beer could taste like for the majority of drinkers in the country.

'[At the start] we had a lot of ambition, but that was to make great tasting beer, not to make the biggest selling craft beer in the UK,' BrewDog co-founder Martin Dickie, tells me. 'We wanted to make exciting beer that we wanted to drink and we were sure that if we did that, then other people would want to drink it too.'

After graduating from Edinburgh's Heriot-Watt University with a master's degree in brewing and distilling, Dickie would join the team at Thornbridge Brewery in Bakewell, Derbyshire, shortly after it was established in 2005. There he would assist in the development of an equally renowned IPA called Jaipur. Two years after this achievement, he would depart Derbyshire, returning home to the north-east of Scotland to start BrewDog with his childhood friend, James Watt.

There's a little bit of mythology that, shortly before he passed away in 2007, the famous beer writer Michael Jackson tasted one of Dickie's prototype BrewDog beers and urged the pair to launch their own brewery. As much as this is true, I've a feeling Watt and Dickie would have set up on their own regardless of what Jackson had told them that fateful night. The first ever batch of Punk IPA was released in April 2007, but despite its ubiquity today, it was far from an instant hit, even with the locals in Aberdeen. 'It was so far away from the kind of beers that people were used to drinking. Plus it was mainly in cask and bottle, and there just weren't many bars equipped to sell cask beer in Aberdeenshire,' Dickie tells me. 'But we were able to get some slow traction, and over the course of that first year it grew from very slow to slightly less slow!'

BrewDog is now the largest independently owned production brewery in the UK and – often questionable marketing activity aside – it largely has its flagship, Punk IPA, to thank for this.

Punk is not the same beer than when I first tried in 2010, however. In fact, that beer was not even the same as the one first released in 2007, as they didn't introduce dry-hopping (the process of adding aromatic hops during or after fermentation) until 2009. Dickie says that this was the biggest change he ever made to the beer, even more so than reducing its alcohol content from 6% to 5.6% in 2011. (It was further reduced again to 5.4% in 2020.) 'We always felt 6% alcohol was really pushing it,' Dickie tells me. 'For what we wanted to be our star beer, it was strong for us, and strong for the [British] market.'

Ask anyone who's been drinking Punk for a long time and they will almost certainly tell you, 'it doesn't taste the same as it used to.' When I quiz him on this, Dickie is remarkably open. Yes, Punk has changed – or rather evolved – many times over the years. First, as they moved from third-party hop suppliers to purchasing their raw ingredients directly from farmers in New Zealand and the USA, and secondly, as they grew so large that certain varieties were no longer available in the vast quantities that they required, and so alternatives had to be sourced.

Punk does not taste like the riotously bitter grapefruit-, mango- and pine resin-infused American West Coast style beer I remember drinking back in 2010. These days it is a mellow beer, predominantly accented with soft notes of apricot and peach. It is also far less bitter than I remember. But this could be a good way of highlighting that, for those of us who have been drinking American-style craft beers for several years, our palates have altered significantly. 'There's more hops in it now than there's ever been,' Dickie says. 'People's perceptions maybe change over time as they become more accustomed to drinking hoppy beer on a regular basis.'

At their gigantic facility in Ellon, around 16 miles north of Aberdeen, Dickie now manages a production team of 120, in which he is still heavily involved. He's now also heavily invested in the technological side of his brewery's efforts to become more sustainable, looking at ways to reduce water usage, and power the whole brewery entirely via sustainable sources, such as wind, and bio-methane produced on site using their own waste material.

Whatever your opinion of BrewDog – and I am confident if you're reading this book that you have one – the effect of their influence, and in particular that of Punk IPA, cannot be overstated. It has, quite literally, helped to define modern British beer as we know it, perhaps more than any other beer in this book. It paved the way for an entirely new generation of breweries by saying 'yes you can make this kind of beer, and in time people will love it.'

Now, as their efforts redouble towards sustainable brewing on a large scale, I hope, at least in this context, that their influence prevails.

Six°North
Auld Toon

Location: Laurencekirk, Aberdeenshire
Style: Belgian Tripel | *ABV:* 9%

The town of Laurencekirk, to the south of Aberdeen, is a long way from Belgium: almost 1200km by road, in fact. But if we're talking in terms of latitude, it's approximately six degrees north. When Robert Lindsay returned to the north-east of Scotland to set up his brewery in 2013, he chose this name not only to signify its connection to the brewing traditions of the country that inspired him, but also to ground it within the Scottish brewing community.

At Six°North Lindsay and his team have channelled the influence and flavours of Belgian beers into something resolutely Scottish. If this sounds a little far-fetched then my advice is to pay a visit to one of their excellent bars scattered throughout Scotland to see, and most importantly, taste, for yourself. Whether it's in the idyllic setting of Stonehaven, sitting across from the harbour with a plate of *frites* (with mayonnaise, as the Belgians do) or in one of their more urban settings, say on Dundee's Union Street or in Aberdeen city centre, I personally assure you, you'll be convinced.

It was in the latter, on a solo trip to the Granite City in early 2015, when I experienced this effortless Belgo-Scottish juxtaposition for myself. Feeling peckish and ordering a traditional Flemish beef carbonnade (served in a bowl made from freshly baked bread, no less), I recall perusing the lengthy tap list looking for something to lend a bit of cut and contrast to the rich and intensely savoury dish. A Pilsner would have been too light, as would a Saison, and the tart acidity of a Flemish Red wasn't what I was in the mood for at that precise moment in time.

After much deliberation I plumped for the brewery's Tripel, Auld Toon, and I was so glad I did. With the weight of its 9% alcohol it had the robustness needed to stand up to the bold, umami-laden flavours of the stew. With every mouthful of dense, fatty, delicious gravy, I washed it down with another sip of beer, finding more to love about it each time I did so. There were spicy aromatics from yeast and hop alike; white pepper, coriander seed, cardamom, all balanced by a fruity, almost apricot-like note. When the stew was gone there was only one thing left to do: I ordered another Tripel.

'Auld Toon reflects where we're from and why we started brewing. Belgian beer has always been at the heart of what we do,' Six°North's Matt Carrington tells me. 'It has a special place in the hearts of our customers. It's big and full of bold flavours but there's a balance and drinkability that keeps people wanting more.'

Fierce Beer
Very Big Moose

Location: Dyce, Aberdeen

Style: Imperial Stout | *ABV:* 12%

Unlike some beer hotspots south of the border, Aberdeen hasn't seen a real explosion of new breweries like in say, London or Manchester, or even Bristol and Newcastle. At one point it was worryingly looking like it would forever remain a one-brewery town. That was until 2016, and the emergence of Fierce Beer, boldly referring it to itself from the off as 'Aberdeen's first microbrewery'. Evidently, the rebellious streak possessed by the brewery (for which the city is now most widely known) has rubbed off.

'Aberdeen is an absolutely cracking town,' Fierce Beer's co-founder, Dave Grant, tells me. 'The breweries that are in or around Aberdeen are doing completely different things. You can wander from one pub to another and not drink the same thing, or even close to it.'

When it launched, Fierce announced itself with a range of beers you could potentially describe as 'wacky'. There was Fuego Feroz, a habanero pepper-infused Pale Ale, Moose Mousse was a Stout brewed with vanilla and cacao, while Cranachan Killer was another Pale, this time designed to mimic the flavours of the popular Scottish dessert. As the brewery matured so did its range of beers, gradually adding more conventional (by Fierce's standards) recipes to their stable. But the desire to push the boundaries of flavour as far as they could possibly go would never leave its system entirely.

Inspired by Yeti, a well-regarded Imperial Stout from Great Divide Brewing of Denver, Colorado, Very Big Moose was designed to be an amped-up version of the aforementioned Moose Mousse. It was brewed in collaboration with the staff at BrewDog's original Aberdeen bar, but where the earlier version of the Stout was a sensible 4.5%, this Imperial version turned out at 12% ABV. It was a monster, and the drinkers of Aberdeen fell head over heels for it at the beer's launch during BrewDog's annual Collabfest.

Well, most people, anyway. 'An interesting fact is that well-known beer writer Matthew Curtis was in Aberdeen for the collabfest launch,' Grant remembers. 'He told us that he had tried the beer, but wasn't a fan of "pastry stouts" and preferred a pint of Bitter.'

That this exchange occurred is true, but it is no longer reflective of my opinion on this beer. While I make no secret of the fact I like beers that are both dry and, yes, bitter, these days I am a very big fan of Very Big Moose. What changed? Well I grew to understand that a lot of people loved this beer even though I didn't (let's think back to the Broad Spectrum of Joy from chapter one) and because of this I returned to the beer in an effort to figure out why that first taste didn't do it for me.

My second experience of this beer was very different. It was like ordering dessert at the end of an indulgent meal even though you already know you've zero room left, but devouring it anyway because it's so delicious. The richness of dark chocolate and cocoa is offset perfectly with indulgent vanilla, then somehow uplifted by the lightness of cinnamon at the end; the latter being the master-stroke that really makes this beer sing. If you can get hold of one of the rare barrel-aged variants – aged in either rum or bourbon casks – this is perhaps even better. But without this original we would have neither. Very Big Moose is a masterclass in modern beer making, taking the concept of deliciousness, and multiplying it to infinity.

Black Isle Blonde

Location: Munlochy, Inverness
Style: Blonde Ale *ABV*: 4.5%

When you think of organic produce, what's the first thing that springs to mind? Maybe some dirt-covered potatoes from the local farmers' market, or perhaps a bunch of vibrantly orange, yellow and purple heritage carrots, emerald green stems still intact as you hoist them from a basket at your local grocer.

There's a solid idea of what organic means in the mind of today's consumer. Presently that thought might not include beer, but it should. Established in 1998 deep in the Highlands beyond Inverness, Black Isle Brewery is committed to its use of completely organic hops and grain, and keeping the impact its production has on the planet to a bare minimum.

'You can't take over the world brewing the kind of beers we do in the way we do, that's not what we are aiming for,' Black Isle's head of operations, Mike Gladwin tells me. 'We have a message we want to get across to people, about the environmental benefits of choosing organic. Blonde, like all our beers, is a vehicle for that message.'

When Black Isle was starting out it needed to produce a beer that would appeal to locals. In the Highlands – a market pretty much devoid of real ale – this meant producing a beer that worked well dispensed via keg. But the brewery also had the desire to send this beer further afield, which meant producing a beer that worked

equally as well served from a cask. Once the intent to create a
beer that suited both formats was established, Blonde was born.

In the late nineties this beer was cutting edge; an ale with
the lightly floral characteristics of noble German hop varieties.
The beer is treated somewhat differently these days, with head
brewer Thorsten Walschek opting to condition the beer in tank
for a minimum of eight weeks, allowing it to carbonate slowly and
naturally. This gives the present-day version of Blonde a softer,
somehow more refreshing character, with notes of lemon rind and
an almost herbaceous crunch of refreshment. I'm lucky enough
to have tried the beer on both cask and keg over the years, with
the former bringing more honey-sweet malt to the fore, and the
extra zing of the latter elevating its citrusy character. More than
twenty years on from its conception, Blonde still tastes and feels as
contemporary as ever, particularly when considering the brewery's
long-term dedication towards a sustainable future for brewers
and drinkers alike.

'Blonde perfectly encapsulates our evolution as a brewery.
As times have changed we've changed as a business to meet
consumer driven demands,' Gladwin says. 'What we haven't
changed is our view that beer we brew should put as little stress
on the environment as possible. As such we are 100% organic,
100% of the time.'

Newbarns
Oat Lager Beer

Location: Leith, Edinburgh
Style: Pale Lager | *ABV:* 4.8%

While it's true that in parts of Scotland you might not find a village local in the traditional English sense, Scotland's cities are home to a thriving bar culture, complete with cultural quirks of its own. One of my favourites being the 'hauf an' hauf', a half pint of beer served alongside a nip of whisky, acceptable to order at any time of the day.

One of the youngest breweries in this book, established as recently as 2019, Newbarns hoped to imprint itself on the bar culture in its home city of Edinburgh with a range of beers you would almost certainly describe as 'pub friendly'. From zesty, yet eminently pint-able Pale Ales to spritzy, refreshing Lagers, Newbarns are the complete package. Its founders also have great pedigree, having collectively been former brewers at Beavertown and The Kernel in London, and Siren in Berkshire. Because of this, a lofty expectation was set from the start.

Unfortunately for Newbarns, the pub culture they sought to capture was taken away from them by the outbreak of the Coronavirus pandemic. This forced them to pivot swiftly from packaging in 50-litre kegs (along with rumoured casks exclusively for the local Edinburgh trade) into cans: lots of cans. Thankfully, they were wise enough to purchase their own canning line, sparing them from being a casualty of the calamity of 2020.

Oat Lager Beer is the perfect example of what Newbarns is about. While this mid-strength Lager almost certainly takes inspiration from the traditional Lagerbiers of Munich and Bavaria, there's a certainly quaffability to it that makes me recall another notable Scottish Lager (one I shall not mention here, but am happy to note comes in bright yellow and red cans, and is popular in bars and music venues alike). Oat Lager Beer is soft and rounded, with light, bready notes wrapped up in a snappy, herbaceous bow. A longing bitterness lingers after every sip, luring you back in for more.

'The idea behind it was to make a Lager that gave the same feeling you get when you drink a Belgain pale [Brasserie de la Senne] like Taras Boulba,' Newbarns co-founder Emma McIntosh tells me. 'The beer has quite a lot going on in terms of the recipe but it's a beer you don't have to necessarily consider and can just enjoy it at face value.'

Less than a year after its inception, Newbarns were voted as the best new brewery in the UK by users of the beer-rating site, Ratebeer. The fact they achieved this during the middle of a global crisis is hugely representative of the gumption possessed by Scottish breweries. I hope by the time this book is published its beer gets a chance to find its sense of place within pubs and bars as originally intended by the brewery. It deserves to, as it's the kind of beer best shared by the pint, with good friends, often and repeatedly.

Pilot
Mochaccino Stout

Location: Leith, Edinburgh
Style: Milk Stout | *ABV*: 5.4%

If rebellion is a signifier of modernity within brewing, what of irreverence? With its feisty, mildly cynical, and often hilarious Twitter account, Leith's Pilot Beer has built a reputation for itself beyond simply the beer it makes. In fact, such is this brewery's notoriety on social media, the word on the street is they might not actually be a brewery at all.

Fear not, however, as I can assure you that, just like the young protagonist in Disney's *Pinocchio* is a real boy, Pilot is very much a real brewery, and one that makes excellent beer. Founders Matt Johnson and Patrick Jones met in 2012 while studying for their master's degrees in brewing and distilling at Edinburgh's Heriot-Watt University. A year later they would establish their brewery in Leith, the port district on Edinburgh's north side, where they remain to this day.

'Having come from UK pub culture, what we never wanted to do when we started Pilot was simply transplant a US craft brewery into Scotland, we wanted to be fresh and modern but with an eye on our roots,' Jones tells me. 'While we were never a traditional real ale brewery we always wanted to keep something of the spirit of the pub about us. While that's something of a nebulous concept, it's far easier to feel than to put into words.'

A beer that embodies this philosophy is Pilot's delectable Mochaccino Stout – or 'Mocha' for short. It's a beer that's wholly representative of the brewery's modern-meets-traditional approach, working just as well on cask as it does straight out of a can. The former is where it really shines for me though, allowing the medley of flavours from its additions of coffee (roasted as per the brewery's specifications), cacao husks and vanilla to shine through.

'We probably only fully realised what Mocha means to our customers when we launched our web shop and saw cases of it flying out,' Jones says. 'That felt like a real vindication of our philosophy; we'd made something undoubtedly modern and bold, but that people wanted to keep coming back to.'

Mochaccino Stout uses the addition of lactose (also known as milk sugar) to give it a full-bodied texture. This ingredient has traditionally been used to make Milk Stouts for many decades, but Mocha is absolutely not your father's (or mother's) beer. Despite its medley of sweet ingredients, the other element to this beer that makes it really shine is restraint. All of the flavours work well in harmony without ever becoming overbearing, allowing you to enjoy the bittersweet combination of chocolate and coffee with immense satisfaction.

As Pilot say, it's a 'rich, comforting pint of luxury'. It also demon- strates that, as impudent as Pilot's online persona may seem, behind the scenes they take what they're doing very seriously indeed.

Vault City
Strawberry Skies

Location: **Portobello, Edinburgh**
Style: **Fruited Sour** | *ABV*: **8.5%**

Initially brewing in Dundee and now based on the north-east side of Edinburgh, Vault City is a relative newcomer to the Scottish scene that quickly found adulation from diehard beer fans. This is largely because while many of its peers were investing in the production of increasingly aromatic IPAs, they turned the tables and – against the laws of commercial sense – decided to focus entirely on the production of expressively acidic and intensely flavourful sour beers.

This immediately made Vault City stand out, which is difficult to do in a nation of well over 2,000 breweries, let alone in a Scottish beer market where Sours are practically the polar opposite to the norm served in most bars. But maybe that's the point. When they arrived on the scene in late 2018, Vault City offered beers that didn't taste like beer. And while they contain enough nuance and complexity to win over a certain breed of enthusiast – myself included – there's also a playful element to what this brewery produces, giving it immediate appeal to folks who think they don't like beer at all. If being modern means removing barriers that prevent some people from enjoying beer, then Vault City are taking to them like a wrecking ball.

Strawberry Skies is a personal favourite because it's demonstrative of both the prowess and quality that Vault City's beers possess, as well as the brewery's innate sense of fun. I recall one particular festival when a glass of this beer was served to me with a fresh strawberry on the rim. Its fruit flavours, precise as a knife edge, dance across your palate with tart notes of strawberry, softened a little with tactful additions of hibiscus and vanilla, before finishing neatly with a rounded, and never shocking, acidity. It's as much a visual treat as it is delicious, too, pouring a vibrant shade of red, and topped with a pinkish foam. Take my advice and try pairing it with a breakfast of bacon and eggs for a weekend treat.

'You shouldn't have to be a brewer or a microbiologist to enjoy these beers,' Vault City's brewer, Andy Gibson tells me. 'Strawberry Skies is an old friend, the mentor who showed you the way, dependable and delightful on the rare occasion you get to meet up again once a year or so.'

Tempest
Long White Cloud

Location: Tweedbank, Borders
Style: New Zealand Pale Ale | *ABV:* 5.4%

An issue with hyperbole is that it can often pull attention away from others who are doing exceptional things. Not to say that those who receive great praise don't deserve it, but this adulation could perhaps, on occasion, be shared more evenly. I see hype, and its sister evil – the fear of missing out – as something of an uncomfortable necessity within modern British beer. It creates a groundswell of fervour, propelling breweries into the limelight and building momentum for the rest of the scene behind it. Sadly, though, this can often result in some spectacular breweries being cast aside in its wake.

This is always how I've felt about Tempest Brewing Co. Established in 2010 in Tweedbank, roughly 25 miles north of the Scottish-English border, it arrived maybe two or three years before the Americanised idea of 'craft beer' in the UK really began to take hold. While breweries in bigger cities were picked up by the wave of interest this generated, Tempest carried on doing their thing without much of the same fanfare.

I will never forget my first bottle of Long White Cloud, Tempest's flagship New Zealand-hopped Pale Ale. It was discovered in my local North London off-licence around late 2010, nestled alongside bottles from The Kernel, but also some other breweries for which the wave of hype was not as merciful, and which no longer exist today. Thankfully, Tempest endured, and that's likely because of the exceptional white grape, passion fruit and herbaceous snap of New Zealand Nelson Sauvin hops that sing like a choir of angels in this beer. At the time I remember thinking it was one of the best beers I had ever tasted, and on revisiting it while researching this book I still consider it to be among the finest modern pales out there.

'When creating a beer we often try to capture a place or a feeling. This approach helps make each beer distinct from the others and speaks to our curiosity and openness about the flavours of the world,' Tempest's head of marketing, Neil Blackburn, tells me. 'The terroir of New Zealand is what we try to capture in this beer each time.'

The beer has changed over the years. Nelson Sauvin, like any agricultural product, does not taste exactly the same year on year, and for a long while it was only available to smaller breweries in limited quantities, with supply far outstripping demand. Tempest compensated for this by subtly tinkering with the recipe over the years, while ensuring that, at its core, this very modern beer was a showcase for the exceptional New Zealand hop variety, harnessing a taste of the Land of the Long White Cloud.

'It's the continual pursuit of excellence that fuels the brewery,' Blackburn continues, 'and getting an extra 1% out of each of our core range beers from one release to the next is what keeps us and the beers evolving.'

Overtone
Ooft!

Location: Yoker, Glasgow
Style: New England Double IPA | *ABV:* 8%

Glasgow is a great city, one of my favourites in the entire world. When I visit I typically stay in Finnieston on the west side, a rapidly gentrifying area that's home to some exciting restaurants, interesting bars, and the serenely picturesque Kelvingrove Park for when you need to walk it all off with a breakfast roll the next morning. The influx of the young and upwardly mobile hasn't quite driven out the classic character of the area, however, with spots such as The Park Bar and The Islay Inn a sound choice if you're in the mood for a more traditional welcome. The Ben Nevis is a particular

favourite bolthole of mine, combining the best of the old world with the new. I pretty much always call in for a 'hauf an' hauf' at the start of a visit.

By my reckoning Glasgow should have one of the most exciting and well-developed beer cultures within the whole of the UK. It's home to Charles Rennie Mackintosh and the famous school of art, and bands such as Belle & Sebastian. But while the influence of this culture can be felt in some of its pubs and bars, the city has not quite been overwhelmed with the raft of new brewing talent that we've seen in other cities like London, Manchester or Bristol. I often find myself scratching my head trying to figure out why. None of the above is to say that Glasgow isn't a great beer town, but if the city's arts and music scenes can be at the cutting edge of popular culture, then so too should its beer.

Which is why I was so pleased when Overtone Brewing arrived on the scene in 2018, adding a breath of fresh air. Its beers are resolutely present tense, largely focusing on hazy, juicy IPAs and bright, spritzy, Fruited Sours, all packed in vibrantly coloured and eminently Instagrammable 440ml cans. They are as much influenced by the most current brewing trends out of the US as they are by what's happening right here in the UK.

Ooft! is one such example; an opaquely yellow Double IPA that deals out handfuls of pineapple and guava, pursued by a little coconut, and finally a lick of orange pith. Such is its tropical character you could arguably stand a cocktail umbrella in it and call it a Pina Colada. It's fun, it's delicious, and it's determinedly untraditional in terms of Glaswegian beer. The name is inspired by a lighthearted take on the local 'Weegie' dialect, onomatopoeically expressing the sound you'll make after taking your first sip.

'We wanted to create a series of beers that related to our home city,' Overtone's Kayley Barbour tells me. 'Glasgow slang has always been a personal favourite of ours, so we decided to create a "lost in translation" series based on Glasgow slang words that nobody really understands, each with a different beer style.'

Harviestoun
Ola Dubh 12

Location: **Alva, Stirling**
Style: **Imperial Porter** | ABV: **8%**

When Harviestoun Brewery was approached by its American importer in the year 2000 asking for a 'wood aged beer' the wheels of fate were well and truly greased. Selecting the brewery's robust Porter, Old Engine Oil – which was developed the year before – master brewer Stuart Cail sourced some ex-Dalmore whisky casks and matured the beer within them for six months. The result, called OEO Special Reserve, sold out quickly. This inspired Cail to do more, but with the desire, as he describes it, to 'take things to the next level.'

In 1997 Cail had developed another beer called Bitter and Twisted. This pale and hoppy Blonde beer might seem almost tame by today's standards, but at the time it was among a growing wave of Pale Ales that were seen as groundbreaking. Bitter and Twisted picked up many awards, including being named as the prestigious CAMRA Champion Beer of Britain at the 2003 Great British Beer Festival. After this victory Cail desired to work with a distiller of similar prestige, and so approached 2003's Distiller of the Year, Highland Park, on the Isle of Orkney.

Working with Highland Park allowed Cail to obtain a range of whisky casks of different ages, and learn how different barrels imparted different flavours within the base beer of Old Engine Oil. When a representative from their US distributor visited the brewery to taste the first release from these barrels his jaw dropped, and he purchased the entire batch. As word about this stunning new whisky barrel-aged beer grew, soon customers in the UK were demanding it, too, and so Ola Dubh (meaning 'Black Oil' in Gaelic) was born.

'There's been a lovely interest in this beer from the beginning and whenever we put new releases they always sell out quickly,' Cail tells me. 'People have laid down various vintages in order to taste them against later releases and also to see how they age. The ratings and feedback we get for Ola Dubh are fantastically positive, which is great to hear.'

I've been lucky to taste many vintages of Ola Dubh over the years, including variants aged in twenty- and thirty-year-old Highland Park barrels. The most commonly found version is aged in barrels that formerly held the distillery's best-selling twelve-year-old impression. What I love about this beer is not only how well it showcases the flavours of whisky in the form of fruit cake, green apple, oak and a little charcoal, but how none of this takes away from the qualities of the Porter. There's dark chocolate, roasted barley and hints of caramel in here, too, but somehow these many

characteristics come together to form something whole. Nothing feels out of place in Ola Dubh, especially if you happen to be adjacent to a log fire, and within a knife's reach of a particularly ripe Scottish Cheddar cheese.

Harviestoun is a remarkable brewery that began breaking the British beer rulebook before James Watt and Martin Dickie had even sat their GCSEs. It's now common to visit a brewery and find a range of different wine and spirit casks full of maturing beer, but at the turn of the century this was a rarity in the UK. Stuart Cail might not be a name as well-known as some who've entered the brewing world more recently, but he's a true pioneer, and his meticulous use of barrels to enhance the flavours of beer forms a great part of his legacy.

'We, along with many brewers in Britain, are independent and we produce everything by hand in small batches. This allows for us to produce top quality beer as well as being innovative in beer styles, which encapsulates the idea of Modern British Beer,' Cail tells me. 'The current range and selection of quality beers now available to the consumer is better than it's ever been in my 30 odd years as a brewer. Long may it continue in these challenging times.'

YORKSHIRE AND THE NORTH-EAST

NEWCASTLE UPON TYNE ● Wylam
Almasty

Durham ♀

Donzoko ♀

Black Sheep ♀

Roosters ♀

Saltaire ♀
Salt Beer Factory

● LEEDS
North
Northern Monk

Mallinsons ♀

Abbeydale
SHEFFIELD ● Kelham Island
Saint Mars of the Desert

Thornbridge ♀

Yorkshire is home to more breweries per capita than any other part of the United Kingdom. Even London, with around 140 breweries, has not yet managed to knock this brewing powerhouse from its lofty mantle. It's one reason why, perhaps, the county carries such a great amount of pride when it comes to its beer. It's home to some of the most interesting breweries in the UK, whether still wet behind the ears or steeped in decades of rich heritage, all are contributing towards its considerable legacy. Pride is also the word that comes to mind when describing the beers and breweries of the North-East, which is why – apart from these regions being geographically adjacent – I made the decision to group them together in this chapter.

I lived in the North-East for a few years. It's here I attended university, although I can't say much of the beer I consumed during this portion of my life left much of an impression, bar the odd stinking hangover. What it did leave me with, before I headed down to London for the next part of my life, was a sense of the quiet dignity with which people from this region carry themselves. Whether I was travelling up for a night on the tiles in Newcastle, or westward to Leeds, there's a sense of kinship here and that's reflected in the beer this region produces.

Beer from Yorkshire and the North-East is keenly distinctive, to a point where it almost typifies a certain stoicism present in the people who call it home. And just like its residents, the personalities of these beers shifts on a hyper-local level, the ales of each region displaying their own varied yet defining characteristics.

A traditional pint of Bitter from North Yorkshire, for example, is bitter in every sense of the word; aggressively so to the uninitiated, but a comforting friend to those who have earned its trust, perhaps by engaging in a lengthy yomp across the moors. The area's hard water lends its beers an astringent, almost flint-like minerality, which is sometimes compensated for by the use of speciality malts, lending them soft copper tones and licks of sweetness. Head west, however, and the beers shift from amber-hued to straw-pale, the far softer water allowing floral and fruity hop notes to shine brightly, but still with a powerful bitterness that jabs at your palate like a prize fighter.

Then move south to Sheffield and towards the Derbyshire border and the beers take on a softer character. A lingering sharpness remains, but this is buffeted by sweeter notes, with a biscuit-like crunch rounded out by a soft, floral aroma. The North-East, and in particular Newcastle, is world famous (or infamous, depending on who you ask) for Brown Ale; darker still and less bitter than the beers of North Yorkshire, but by no means less distinctive.

Admittedly I'm generalising a little here, but when I spoke earlier in this book about regionality being a defining characteristic of modern British beer, this is exactly the kind of thing I was referring to. Beer in a modern sense is about turning away from a march towards uniformity, and ensuring its flavours and aromas establish a deep sense of place in the drinker. You will notice variances like these in similar beer styles brewed throughout the entirety of the UK, but nowhere else does this seem so obvious as it does in Yorkshire and the North-East.

The beer produced here is so distinctive because its makers want you to know immediately that you're drinking northern beer. As the culture of beer in the UK continues to shift and change, I predict that brewers will increasingly look to define themselves by embracing aspects of flavour that are strongly representative of their region. But if you want to experience right now what the future for modern beer across the whole of the UK might look like in the not too distant future, head north.

Wylam
Jakehead

Location: Newcastle upon Tyne
Style: American IPA | *ABV:* 6.3%

Over the past decade the city of Newcastle upon Tyne has become a hotspot for some of the most exciting pubs, breweries and beer festivals in the UK. It's no coincidence that the beer enthusiasts who call it home have modestly bestowed it with the title 'The Capital of Craft'. One of the people responsible for the city becoming such a hub for great beer is former nightclub owner and music promoter-turned-director of Wylam Brewery, Dave Stone.

Established in 2000, 10 miles east of Newcastle city centre, in a village of the same name, Wylam began life as a very traditional family owned brewery. Founders John Boyle and Robin Leighton, and latterly Boyle's son, Matt, made a name for themselves locally with beers such as Gold Tankard Ale and Landlord's Choice, a far cry from the distinctly contemporary beers the brewery is known for today.

Tired of the music business, but excited about the future prospects of British beer, Stone, who had also been running a couple of pubs where Wylam's real ales were popular, became involved with the brewery in 2012, along with business partner Rob Cameron. In 2015 Stone would become its managing director, and increased his efforts in pulling the brewery in a very different direction, away from tradition and towards modernity. This culminated in 2016 when Wylam relocated to the Grade II-listed Palace of Arts in

Newcastle's Exhibition Park (the building was originally constructed for the Great North East Exhibition of 1929). Now reborn as a brewery, it's seen Stone return to his roots; it also serves as a live music venue, as well as hosting the annual Craft Beer Calling festival.

Wylam is now well known by beer lovers around the UK for a range of beers that cross modern English brewing with distinctly North American influences. One beer in particular serves as a marker of this brewery's remarkable transformation, Jakehead IPA, which has become the brewery's lynchpin since it was developed in 2012 by head brewer Ben Wilkinson when he joined the brewery. Remarkably, it was the first IPA the brewery ever released.

'Like everything we do here we brewed it because we want to drink it. That's our watchword,' Stone explains. 'With Ben's interest in this beer style and its history, and considering Wylam's traditional origins, he designed a hybrid with the malt backbone of a traditional British IPA fused with the US take on the style.'

Just like the brewery itself, Jakehead is not a beer that has stood still. Earlier iterations had a deep copper appearance, with pin-bright clarity that showed off its lustre, while fruit cake and malt loaf flavours melded effortlessly with hop notes of pithy grapefruit. Over time, however, the beer has become a touch less bitter and taken on a slightly lighter appearance, with elements of tropical fruit creeping in, augmenting with its citrusy personality. Like the brewery that spawned it, Jakehead has found its resting place between old and new. What is modernity if it doesn't respect its own tradition? It's a question that's summed up in every sip of this fruity, zesty, comforting beer.

'Let's face it, without learning during the journey there is nothing to propel you forward,' Stone says. 'For the modern beer drinker the importance of the evolution of the journey and, as part of it, the evolution of beer is and always should be sacrosanct.'

Almasty
Kush

Location: Newcastle upon Tyne
Style: New England Double IPA   ABV: 8%

As modern breweries have become increasingly reliant on the deeply aromatic and intensely flavourful hop varieties from places like Australia, New Zealand and the USA, so too has the beer drinker's lexicon had to expand in order to describe them. As with the beers themselves, these changes have not always sat easily among the hardiest of traditionalists. As a writer, I understand that tasting notes can be jarring to those unaccustomed to them, but also feel a certain duty to describe beers in a way that triggers thirst and excitement, and ensuring my vocabulary remains up to date when doing so.

'Dank' is one of the more recent descriptors to appear in the beer writer's thesaurus. In the historic British sense, it was used to describe damp, miserable and unpleasant spaces; a cramped and mouldy cellar, perhaps, or a rain-soaked alleyway caked with rotting autumn leaves. It almost certainly does not bring to mind the image of a frothy, golden pint, with pungent citrus and tropical fruit aromas.

In the US, and more recently in the UK, however, dank is used to describe a very specific aroma – that of the intensely heady scents produced by compounds called terpenes, existent in a not-so distant relative of the hop flower known as cannabis. Terpenes are present in hops too, and are highly volatile. When exposed to heat they evaporate, but when hops are added to beer during or after fermentation, in a process called dry-hopping, they remain suspended in the finished beer. It's due to their innate sensitivity that many brewers implore you to keep beer cold, and drink it as fresh as possible.

Aromatically, modern hop varieties including, but not limited to, Simcoe, Mosaic, Centennial and Columbus share an incredibly similar aroma with certain strains of cannabis. This is why 'dank' has crept in as such a popular descriptor when talking about modern beer styles, and I can't think of a better word to describe Kush, a Double IPA brewed in the New England style from Newcastle's Almasty Brewing Co. It's no coincidence the beer is named after a very popular (at least, allegedly so) strain of cannabis developed in the early nineties.

On first encountering this beer your olfactory system will be engulfed by pungent aromas of overripe mango. There's a little pine resin in there too, though, and perhaps a touch of candied orange peel creeping around the edges. On tasting, you'll be further pulled into a mire of passion fruit, pineapple, melon and lychee. There is a degree of restraint, however, in that these flavours peak gently, before softly fading into the background, not giving away an iota of this beer's 8% ABV. One can of Kush and I guarantee you'll be reaching into the back of your record collection searching for those old Pink Floyd LPs.

Donzoko
Big Foam

Location: Hartlepool, County Durham
Style: Pale Lager | ABV: 5%

Reece Hugill is a charming young man. Still in his twenties, he runs his brewing operation, Donzoko, entirely by himself. But these are not the beers of some upstart looking to make a quick buck in a booming beer industry. No, this is a brewer who carries himself with all the air and grace of a veteran Bavarian brewmaster. And from his home in Hartlepool, by the mouth of the River Tees, he produces some of the most exciting contemporary Lagers in the UK today.

While his Munich-style beer, Northern Helles, forms the mainstay of his production, Big Foam is more an expression of his art. It's also incredibly popular with his brewery's fans on social media, and has become the subject of several memes within certain circles of the internet.

'I spent the first two years of Donzoko trying to perfect Northern Helles,' Hugill tells me. 'I began thinking about how I could distill this character, and amplify it into a true representation of what Donzoko Lager is; something bolder and a bit of a statement. Lager that's a bit dishevelled, with character. Lager that's a bit more "rustic".'

At the time he'd also been researching the history of beer in Teesside, particularly, the hyper-local phenomenon known as 'banked beer'. Historically, in order to satisfy the post-work arrival of local steelworkers en masse, publicans would part pour as many pints as possible, before storing them in the fridge, and then topping them up before serving. This would result in the formation of an almost comical amount of foam, settling, quiff-like, at the top of the glass. 'My family had worked in the steelworks for generations, before it closed in 2015,' Hugill continues. 'The name was a nice tribute to that tradition. Plus, foam is the best part of beer.'

As well as being a nice tribute to the local beer traditions of the region, Big Foam has the nature to match its name. On pouring, a torrent of off white, tightly compacted bubbles rapidly form on top of the beer, releasing grassy, peach-scented aromas from German Hallertau Blanc hops, along with an Australian variety known as Astra. Big Foam builds its flavour on a foundation of German malts, plus a locally grown heritage variety of wheat called Spelt. The latter adds a dryness to the biscuit-sweet base layer, before the hops introduce flavours of white grape and melon.

There's also a subtle acidity, which seems to enhance the beer's inherent characteristics in a way that's a little like turning the contrast up on your television. This is thanks to a small addition of lactic acid, which Hugill produces naturally at the brewery using his own culture of bacteria, and is a method adapted from traditional German brewing. 'Rustic' can be a difficult term to use in the description of beer, but you'd almost certainly use it yourself after sipping a Big Foam.

'I don't think you could taste the bright hops, bready malt and acidic twang and confuse it with another UK brewery's Lager,' Hugill adds. 'Whether it's to your taste or not, it's something I'm quite proud of. It's just a big ol' foamy pint of Lager, and really should be enjoyed solely on that pretense, by everyone!'

*

Just before this book was published Donzoko announced that it would be relocating the brewery to Leith, Edinburgh. Although, Hugill has assured me his beers shall remain resolutely Northeastern in spirit.

Durham
Temptation

Location: Bowburn, County Durham
Style: Russian Imperial Stout | ABV: 10%

The origin story of Durham Brewery is one that's often repeated in contemporary brewing lore; that of a homebrewer whose unbridled enthusiasm for beer transformed a relatively innocent hobby into a fully fledged career. For brewery co-founder Steve Gibbs, this tale began in 1977, when he was inspired to take up homebrewing after a visit to the nascent Great British Beer Festival, taking place that year at Alexandra Palace in North London.

It would be almost another two decades before he and his wife, Christine, would set up a brewery of their own, with Gibbs eventually relocating from Kent to the North-East, where they'd establish Durham Brewery in 1994. A producer cherished by those in the know for its striking modern-meets-traditional beers, the brewery is perhaps best known for its remarkable Temptation Imperial Stout.

'Our identity was connected from the beginning to Durham, the cathedral and Celtic artwork,' Gibbs tells me. 'Temptation is one of our oldest beers and fits this identity perfectly. The early image worked because I remember delivering beer to a pub in Bradford to be told that it was made by monks in Durham.'

Like the beginnings of Durham Brewery itself, the origins of Temptation stretch right back to Gibbs' days as a homebrewer. In 1978 he purchased a copy of Dave Line's *Brewing Beers Like Those You Buy*, within which was the author's interpretation of the recipe for the legendary Courage Imperial Russian Stout. This was a beer revered by Gibbs, who was living in the south-east at the time, where Courage-owned pubs were still commonplace.

'Imperial Russian Stout was never visible at the bar, you had to ask for it,' he recalls. 'The little bottle held the biggest beer ever, enough for a small sipping glass, and I still believe there to be nothing like it, even now.'

Despite its connections to Gibbs' origins as a brewer, Temptation wouldn't join the brewery's line-up until several years after it was established. In its early days the brewery's output was solely via cask, and he feared a beer of this strength might not be well suited to such a high-volume format. This changed in 2000, when the brewery upgraded its facility with a larger mash tun so that it could brew stronger beers more easily, and added a bottling line so it could also package them in a format more suitable to their strength.

Gibbs encountered another hurdle when it came to naming this new beer, as he wanted to bestow a title in tribute to the Courage beer that inspired it. However, in their acquisition of Courage in 1995, brewing giants Scottish and Newcastle (now part of Dutch-multinational Heineken) had also picked up the trademark for 'Russian Imperial Stout', despite ending the production of the beer in question.

'Not wishing a lawsuit I looked for a new name,' Gibbs tells me. 'One of my favourite beers is [Hoegaarden] Verboden Vrucht (a strong Belgian-style ale, its name translating as "Forbidden Fruit") and the name Temptation seemed obvious. We had already aligned the beer names with Durham and its cathedral, so this seemed appropriate. A trademark search showed the name to be owned by Marston's, who sold it to us.'

Now in production for almost two decades, Temptation is a beer of supreme delectation. Such is its class that I won't judge if you feel like donning your finest three-piece or ballgown before the ceremony of opening, pouring and sipping begins. Its aroma of black treacle and heavily roasted coffee can be sensed from three feet away, and to taste it is like guzzling rich molasses, with moments of hazelnut, burnt toffee and chocolate cake. All of which leads to a remarkably clean, dry finish, ensuring this beer works as well when paired with food as it does on its own. Might I recommend a rich beef or mushroom stroganoff, or, if you're pushed for time, a hunk of blue cheese the size of your fist should suffice.

'There is very good loyalty to this beer. I have even been told that it is the best beer ever made,' Gibbs says, modestly. 'I think it represents the stability and quality of the brewery.'

Roosters
Yankee

Location: Harrogate, North Yorkshire
Style: American Pale Ale | *ABV*: 4.3%

By today's standards, Rooster's Yankee, first brewed in 1993, might seem a little retro to some palates. Straw-pale in the glass, its distinctive grapefruit scent is immediate and obvious, drawing you in to take deep, comforting sips, and enjoy its tones of citrus, wrapped in just a hint of honey-sweet malt, before leading you to a rasping, mineral finish: the former telling of its North American influences, the latter, its deep North Yorkshire roots.

'Despite the beer having always been brewed with four simple, yet very specific ingredients – soft Yorkshire water, English pale malt, American Cascade hops and Rooster's house yeast strain – the perception of Yankee has naturally and gradually changed over the years,' Rooster's commercial director, Tom Fozard, says. 'Especially over the past decade as more aggressively hopped beers have become more mainstream and sub-styles of beers have been created, resulting in a shift in consumer expectations.'

Rooster's has been under the stewardship of Ian Fozard and his twin sons, Tom and Oliver (who serves as head brewer), since they acquired the brewery in 2011. Together they have ushered it into the modern brewing age through well-considered expansion and thoughtful rebranding, presenting itself as something that is very much in fitting with the brewing culture of today, while also being true to its origins. The brothers Fozard have also furthered the

brewery's American influences, inspired by their own repeated trips to the United States. Today they are as well known for distinctively modern beers such as Baby Faced Assassin IPA, and Pils-near, a Lager/ale hybrid, as they are for stone-cold classics like Yankee.

In terms of brewing history in the UK, without Yankee, none of what came after might have come to pass. Not just for Rooster's itself, but for modern British brewing as a whole. The brewery was originally founded in 1993 by one Sean Franklin. He had made his name a decade before with the eponymously named Franklin's Brewery, which closed down in the mid-1980s. Before he established Rooster's, Franklin had gotten wind of an American-made pale beer that was becoming popular due to its remarkably punchy grapefruit character, provided by a then relatively unknown hop variety (in the UK at least) called Cascade. The beer in question was Sierra Nevada Pale Ale, produced by the Northern California brewery of the same name.

Developed by homebrewer-turned-industry phenomenon Ken Grossman, it's remarkable to think how a beer, based on a classic English Pale Ale recipe, but hopped with a distinctively American-tasting variety, would influence the course of brewing on a global scale. For Franklin, getting hold of whole-flower Cascade hops meant bypassing English hop merchants and specially importing them so he could impart its powerful citrus characteristics into his own beers.

'Yankee led the way for British brewing by being truly unique,' Tom Fozard says. 'Drawing from Sean's past experience of winemaking, and taking advantage of Harrogate's soft water, the emphasis of the beer has always been about allowing the aromatic qualities of the Cascade hop to be front and centre.'

While Sierra Nevada Pale Ale is perhaps the most influential beer in terms of modern beer on a global scale, Yankee might be the same for beer in the UK, and for cask beer in particular. I can think of very few breweries focused on the production of real ale today that don't have a US-hopped, sessionable Pale Ale in their line-up, and Yankee is almost certainly the originator. One challenger to this claim could be a chap called Brendan Dobbin, who applied similar influences to his lauded Yakima Grande Pale Ale. Unlike Rooster's, however, Dobbin's Manchester-based West Coast Brewing Company is no longer in operation.

That Rooster's occupies the space it does today is as much testament to the early influence of Sean Franklin and his desire to bring new flavours and experiences to British beer drinkers as it is to the tenacity and ambition of the Fozards. Walking the tightrope between heritage and innovation is a difficult challenge, but is surely one of the great signifiers of modernity within British brewing culture. Yankee is still the brewery's best-selling cask beer to this day, and is now exported throughout the world, as well as all over the UK.

'Yankee is enjoyed by people now in their sixties and seventies who have been drinking it for several decades, as much as it is by younger drinkers who are setting out on the voyage of beer discovery,' Fozard says. 'It's a modern Pale Ale that's capable of being both a gateway beer and a conjurer of Proustian memories.'

Black Sheep
Black Sheep Ale

Location: **Masham, North Yorkshire**

Style: **English Bitter** | ABV: **4.4%**

Stories of rebellion against cultural norms appear regularly amid the histories of some of the most compelling British breweries. However, rebellion alone isn't a facet of what I feel constitutes the make-up of modern British beer, hence it not appearing in my definition. Instead, I see rebellion as more of a catalyst, one that has been essential in getting beer in the UK to the space it occupies now, but which is no longer representative of our modern beer culture.

One of the original rebels of modern beer as we know it is Paul Theakston, a fifth-generation brewery owner and member of the great Theakston Brewery lineage that began brewing in its home of Masham, North Yorkshire, in 1827. He became managing director at the storied family business aged just twenty-three, taking over from his father, Frank, in 1968. In a twist of events, he would part ways with Theakston Brewery in 1988, a year after brewing giant Scottish and Newcastle (now a part of Heineken) came calling with its chequebook.

Despite leaving this great legacy behind, his business in Masham was far from over. Theakston would acquire a building previously owned by the North Yorkshire Malt Roasting Company. A part of the original (and now long gone) Lightfoot's Brewery, which is also tied into his family brewing history, the site is located just a few hundred metres from Theakston Brewery. Here he would

establish his own brewery, Black Sheep, which produced its first beers in September 1992.

Appointing Paul Ambler – formerly of McMullen's in Hertfordshire – as head brewer, the fledgling Black Sheep developed two initial recipes designed to distance itself from Theakston beers such as Old Peculier, which is known for the strong, fruity character created by its house yeast strain. The first of these was an eponymously named Best Bitter destined for the pub trade, while the second was designed for what was, for the time, an exciting emerging retail category known as Premium Bottled Ale. Enter the rebel: Black Sheep Special Ale.

'The level of quality out there was really crap,' Paul's son, Jo Theakston, who today is Black Sheep's sales and marketing director, tells me. 'The whole thing about what we were doing at the time in terms of kicking against the norm, and what was going on was all about quality, because there was a real lack of it in the industry at that moment.'

Jo and his older brother, Rob, now the brewery's managing director, took over the day-to-day running of the brewery from their dad in 2011, before his eventual retirement in 2018. He recalls how in the early nineties there was a deliberate intention to disrupt this emerging category by producing a beer that used only the highest quality of ingredients, from Maris Otter barley malt to whole-flower English hops, and then giving the bottle striking branding that played on Black Sheep's heritage, while still standing out from the crowd. 'When you put it in the context of the craft beer movement it maybe feels a bit underwhelming,' Theakston continues. 'But at the time it was quite a step forward.'

The beer was a hit, eventually growing to become one of the top ten selling bottled premium ales in the UK. It's soft balance of subtly sweet malts and floral hops accompanied by a tremendous, bracing astringency, the presence of the latter a result of the brewery's use of traditional Yorkshire squares – open-top fermentation vessels made of solid slate. This character gives Black Sheep Ale remarkable thirst-quenching properties, even more so if taken immediately after a brisk stroll across the surrounding Yorkshire Dales.

The beer eventually made its way into pubs, too, albeit simply known as 'Special Ale', with its red pump clip designed to stand apart from the signature green of Black Sheep Bitter. At some point in the beer's history the 'special' was dropped, becoming known simply as Black Sheep Ale. Although, Jo Theakston admits, a level of confusion has always persisted between it and Black Sheep Bitter.

'Blame my dad on this. Traditionally you'd build a brand with the same beer, but us being a bit odd, we managed to do it with two completely separate beers,' he tells me. 'It's that Black Sheep approach to it I guess, which gives it an edge. It reflects our heritage and what we have – which is quite a bit different to a lot of brewers out there.'

Northern Monk
Faith

Location: **Leeds, West Yorkshire**
Style: **New England Pale Ale** | *ABV:* **5.4%**

According to owner and founder Russell Bisset, when he establish-ed Northern Monk brewery in July 2013 he had just £5,000 set aside to launch his startup. This amount would've barely got a brewery off the ground in 1993, let alone two decades later. Thanks to his particular brand of northern stoicism, however, he was able to get his fledgling business up and running, initially by brewing itiner-antly at facilities near to his hometown of Bradford.

Thanks to a lot of gumption and a little bit of, well, faith, a year later he was able to secure a premises for the brewery at the stunning Old Flax Store, a former mill and Grade II-listed building on the outskirts of Leeds city centre. All at once it imbued a distinct sense of place to the delicious, forward-thinking beers his brewery had already begun to produce.

Almost a decade on, it feels apt that a beer called Faith has become Northern Monk's best-selling flagship, although it may surprise you to hear it was never planned to be. This deliberately hazy, exquisitely juicy beer, distinctive thanks to its heady blend of overripe mango and zesty citrus flavours, buoyed by a soft, pillowy mouthfeel and subtly dry finish, didn't initially join the Northern Monk line-up until 2015. It was created as a celebration of a North American hop variety known as Citra, which Bisset tells me he was 'particularly excited about'.

TRUE
NORTH

NORTHERN
MONK

Fate, however, was destined to throw a spanner in the works. 'Faith was to be our all Citra Pale Ale. We loved it,' Bisset tells me. 'However, by batch three we were told by our supplier there was to be no more Citra.' Though it is now the most cultivated hop variety in the world, in 2015 demand for Citra still far outstripped supply. This was before Northern Monk was established enough to contract its hop supply in advance, and before it had built the direct relationships it enjoys today with hop merchants in the Pacific Northwest. Faith, it seemed, was down, but true to Bisset's determined nature, it was not out. In spring 2017, following a pilgrimage to some trailblazing breweries in New England, Bisset and Northern Monk's long-time head brewer, Bryan Dickson, were inspired to return to the recipe.

They decided to introduce the Mosaic and Columbus hop varieties to the regular supply of Citra they had now secured, adding a dank, resinous edge to the beer's intensely juicy flavour. Meanwhile, the grain bill was tweaked to accommodate wheat and oats alongside barley, to give the beer the soft, rounded character it's become admired for. Sliding into the brewery's core range as an outsider, the beer was an instant hit, quickly helping them grow into a nationally distributed brand.

'The beer is a mashup of our favourite British cask ales from early inspirations like Timothy Taylor's Landlord to the likes of Fyne Ales Jarl, Oakham Citra and Marble Pint,' Bisset says. 'We wanted to take the balance and sessionability born from the pint drinking culture in Britain and combine that with inspiration from across the pond.'

'Our brewery's identity is born from the grim up North, pint half full, make the best of it mentality we try to embody,' he adds. 'Faith is at the centre of that.'

North
Triple Fruited Gose

Location: Leeds, West Yorkshire
Style: Fruited Gose | *ABV*: 4.5%

Having established the legendary Leeds beer destination North Bar in 1997, North Brewing founders John Gyngell and Christian Townsley know the way to a beer lover's heart. Fondly referred to as the UK's 'first ever craft beer bar' by many, the pair introduced the unwitting drinkers of Yorkshire to German Lager and Weissbier, strong Belgian ales, trailblazing American breweries that triggered a global brewing revolution, and, more recently, the pioneers of the British craft beer movement.

They also know how to get a party started. Whether it's at their pop up, the Lowlands-themed Atomium bar at the annual Leeds International Beer Festival, or through the infamous weekly 'Tequila Tuesdays' night at North Bar, Townsley and Gyngell understand the way to revellers' hearts is through great hospitality. It's a sense that's also characteristic of their brewery, which they established in 2015 after two decades of building a mini pub empire in Leeds. You'll find the same warm welcome at their city centre taproom as you will at any of their bars, or even their flagship Springwell brewery site. The latter, announced in late 2020 and located towards the north of the city, is capable of hosting up to 500 thirsty beer lovers.

'At North our roots are in hospitality,' Townsley says. 'We brew beer because of its ability to bring people together, prompt shared experiences, and take people on a journey of styles and flavours.'

You could pick out almost any beer from North's line-up to represent their influence on the scene today, with their striking branding from local designer James Ockleford channelling its jovial spirit through striking colours and geometric imagery. Although one beer in particular captures North's inherent party spirit, as well as the brewery's tendency to flip its influences on their head: Triple Fruited Gose.

'Our Triple Fruited Gose series plays a part in opening drinkers up to a new journey of flavours, forcing them to reassess their pre-existing ideas on what a beer can be,' Gyngell tells me. 'Just as with introducing commercial Lager drinkers to their first German Pils in North Bar, Triple Fruited Gose has introduced countless "non beer drinkers" to fun, interesting beer.'

Arriving in an array of constantly changing fruit flavours, such as raspberry and pear, passion fruit and mango, blueberry and lingonberry, each variation is a Mardi Gras of fruit flavours cavorting on your tongue with just enough acidity to keep all of its sweetness in check. Is it even a beer? Absolutely! Is it actually a Gose? Well, it's doubtful.

A traditional Gose (pronounced go-zer) originates from the German town of Goslar, although its spiritual home is arguably Leipzig. A soft, effervescent style of wheat beer, Gose is produced in a way that gives it a naturally light sourness, and is typically flavoured using only coriander seed, but also contains salt, lending a touch of salinity to the finish. The few surviving traditional German versions absolutely do not contain levels of fruit puree that would likely turn the cheeks of the most ardent purists puce in their righteous fury.

Such is the irreverence of North Brewing. They are here to entertain us, and make us feel welcome. To do that requires triggering joy in an ever-growing, more varied range of people. With its Triple Fruited Gose they achieve that effortlessly. If beer is meant to be fun, then this beer is a giant bouncy castle, and everyone's invited.

Saltaire
Triple Choc

Location: **Saltaire, West Yorkshire**
Style: **Stout** | *ABV:* **4.8%**

Situated in the north of the Greater Bradford Metropolitan District, next to the town of Shipley, Saltaire is a perfectly preserved Victorian model village that's home to the impressive Salts Mill building. Now an art gallery, it houses one of the largest permanent collections from famous modern artist and Yorkshireman, David Hockney. I fondly remember visiting the gallery on a school field trip many years ago, and how seeing Hockney's work in the flesh for the first time changed the way I think and feel about art forever.

Now that I feel the same way about beer, it's fortunate that Saltaire is also home to the eponymous brewery, which has been impressing beer fans with its delectable contemporary-meets-traditional beers since it was established in 2003. I've always felt Saltaire to be part of a select group of breweries that falls between the cracks left by the traditional regional breweries that came before them, and those of the craft beer boom that began to appear in their droves around 2010.

I can only imagine how relentlessly frustrating it must've been for the emerging breweries of the late nineties and early 2000s when their gradual efforts to update the face of British brewing were almost lost under a fresh wave of hyperbole that washed up on our shores. With hindsight, however, I feel this may have bestowed some of these breweries with an advantage. They have a foot in both

camps, to a certain degree, an ability to produce beers that appeal to both traditionalists and those who live on the bleeding edge.

Saltaire's Triple Choc is a great example of this; a beer that on its surface is simple, satisfying and comforting, with an ABV that ensures even a diehard enjoyer of real ale won't mind enjoying several within a single sitting. Beneath this, however, for those who care to dive deeper, complexity awaits. Nuanced expressions of dark chocolate form in layers, lending a touch of sweetness that's underpinned by a measured bitterness from English Fuggles hops. Delve further still and you might also taste freshly roasted coffee, with just a hint of liquorice rounding out the detail. Another remarkable characteristic of this beer is that it works surprisingly well paired with spicy food, its bittersweetness taking the edge off chilli heat, without being overpowering.

'We've always been willing to take traditional styles of beer and find new ways of making them interesting,' Saltaire's Nick Helliwell tells me. 'Triple Choc is a great example of that; we were putting flavoured adjuncts in beer long before it became "cool" to do so!'

Salt Beer Factory
Jute

Location: **Saltaire, West Yorkshire**
Style: **Session IPA** | *ABV:* **4.2%**

What is a so-called Session IPA if not a modern-day incarnation of the classic English Bitter? As a style descriptor, if I'm honest, it's one I'm not keen on. For me the term 'IPA' should indicate a beer that is both strong in alcohol and robust in character, not one that falls into the categories of 'light' and 'sessionable'. Semantics aside, the Session IPA has been a breakout category of the past few years, clearly indicating to consumers that these particular beers are both low in strength and redolently hoppy – just as a classic West Yorkshire Pale Ale should be.

Salt Beer Factory's Jute is one such beer. Born from parent company Ossett Brewery, when Salt was launched in 2018 it represented more than £1.7 million worth of investment and three years of planning. Establishing itself in a Grade II-listed former Edwardian tramshed within the UNESCO heritage village of Saltaire, the facility and its adjoining taproom epitomises the image of the modern craft brewery: all glowing neon and shining stainless steel – a vast departure from the traditional structure that surrounds it.

Led by head brewer Colin Stronge, whose own pedigree includes tenures at Marble, Black Isle and Buxton breweries, Salt's range looks and tastes incredibly modern, proudly wearing its North American influences on its sleeve. With its inherent drinkability, however, Jute lends a touch of West Yorkshire quality to a beer with an overtly US character.

'The initial inspiration for Jute was what we call a "pub beer" – beers that are session strength that you can enjoy a few of,' Salt's managing director, Dr Nadir Zairi, tells me: 'Our core beers are named after textiles as a nod to the heritage of Saltaire. Jute as a textile is one of the most accessible and versatile fabrics in the world. Similarly, the goal of our session IPA was to brew an accessible beer, suitable for all occasions.'

Pouring a touch on a hazy side, Jute has a distinctly modern grain bill. Barley malt is accompanied by wheat and oats, the latter giving it a soft, yet full body despite its relatively low strength. The hop bill is no less complex, combining Mosaic and Centennial varieties from the US with Topaz and Vic Secret from Australia, bringing with it notes of ripe melon, passion fruit, lemon zest, and a touch of astringency that's akin to biting into a fresh lychee. What's impressive about this beer is how well these flavours work together. And while it's not quite as bitter as a traditional West Yorkshire Pale Ale, there's just enough at the back end to keep you puckered for another sip.

'We want to bring more people into the world of hop-forward beer,' Zairi adds. 'Jute is the first step in that, from the accessibility of the style down to the recognisability and simplicity of the branding, it is all about brewing a beer that can stand out and be loved by all.'

Mallinsons
Citra

Location: Huddersfield, West Yorkshire
Style: American Pale Ale | *ABV:* 3.8%

There's a certain delight to be had when spotting a Mallinsons clip while perusing a range of hand pulled cask ales. As a Londoner of fifteen years, it wasn't something I saw often, except on occasional jaunts to the North. This meant that when I do unexpectedly come across its beers in the wild, the feeling sets every hair along my arms upright in gleeful anticipation. This is because Mallinsons is a producer of beers with a rare quality, and it's one you'll most likely experience through its range of single-hopped, cask Pale Ales. The sight of its branding is only trumped by a freshly poured pint of its Citra Pale Ale (pulled through a sparkler, as best befits this beer), gleaming bright as a solar flare, and topped with a dense, frothy head of foam.

There are many beers in this book that set their foundations on the cherished Citra hop variety, but few breweries have made the variety their own like Huddersfield's Mallinsons brewery. While their take on this ingredient manages to capture the distinctive zesty grapefruit and tropical mango character so deeply cherished by brewers and drinkers alike, this is not a one note beer. It's remarkably well structured, the presence of barley malt is felt immediately on tasting, despite the beer's almost ghostly paleness, lending a subtle biscuity note that prevents the hops from overpowering your senses.

This gives the beer a certain level of restraint. If the generous addition of Citra in this beer is a 40-piece orchestra, then its malt is the conductor, creating rhythm and melody, all leading to an astoundingly bitter crescendo that will have you leaping to your feet with applause, before heading straight back to the bar for another round.

'For us using a single hop showcases the essence of that variety. We are all about the hops,' brewery co-founder Tara Mallinson tells me. 'People may think that brewing a single-hopped beer is easy, but getting the balance correct and having no place to hide behind malt or yeast requires a lot of finesse. Citra is a dream to work with.'

Abbeydale Brewery

Abbeydale
Daily Bread

Location: Sheffield, South Yorkshire
Style: English Bitter | *ABV:* 3.8%

Sheffield deserves a reputation as one of the best beer cities in the whole of the UK. Often, however, it's overlooked for nearby siblings such as Leeds or Manchester. Why is this? Perhaps it's the quiet, confident nature of its beer-drinking citizens. They know they're sitting on something good, but it's up to outsiders to put in that extra effort and find out just *how* good.

Abbeydale Brewery, based just off the road of the same name to the south of the city centre, has been setting the standard for modern beer in Sheffield since 1996. Founders Pat and Sue Morton immediately wanted to distance themselves from the 'boring brown beers' (their words) that were familiar to locals at the time. Inspired by pioneers such as Brendan Dobbin at the West Coast Brewing Company and Sean Franklin at Roosters, they focused heavily on producing pale, hoppy beers like Absolution, Last Rites, and their flagship, Moonshine.

'In 1996 we saw a need to differentiate from national brands which were almost all brown beers,' Pat and Sue tell me. 'So the brewery started brewing pale beers and built our reputation on them.'

While the couple explain that their traditional best bitter, Daily Bread, isn't particularly representative of them as a brewery (in fact they describe it as an 'outlier'), they do tell me that it was born out of a desire to satisfy the needs of local drinkers. In 2005 the brewery acquired its first pub, The Rising Sun, in the Sheffield suburb of Nether Green. To the couple's dismay, the best-selling beer here was John Smith's, a celebrated brand originating from the Yorkshire town of Tadcaster – although it is now under the ownership of Heineken.

Unable to convert these diehard drinkers to their pale and hoppy range, they began to do a little market research. Sue would put on a varying range of brown Bitters from other local breweries, all the while quizzing those who would order them on what they liked or disliked about each particular beer. Once they had something of a complete picture, they took this information back to the brewery and created their own brown Bitter, Daily Bread.

'Most of the John Smith's drinkers converted happily,' Sue tells me. 'While a significant number went to Brimstone, our American hopped brown ale, and a few went to another pub for a sulk, almost all came back.'

While the couple play down this beer, I feel this story is representative of what makes Abbeydale Brewery, and the Sheffield beer scene as a whole, so special. They could have just as easily told the locals that they would be replacing their beloved Bitter with beers that are closer to what Pat and Sue see as their brewery's ideal. But instead they decided to listen to the community and create a beer for everyone to enjoy; a beer that's deep-copper in colour, with an aroma of ground rye, caramel and white pepper. Sipping reveals a character of toasted bread and caraway seed, with just a lick of citrusy zing, hinting that English Fuggles hops are joined by Columbus from America, and Bobek from another major hop growing nation, Slovenia.

'It's a simple beer,' Pat says. 'But our emphasis as with everything we make is on making sure it's the best it can be, which makes it a great representation of the best bitter style.'

Saint Mars of the Desert
Jack D'Or

Location: **Sheffield, South Yorkshire**
Style: **Saison** | *ABV:* **5.8%**

What could a beer originally conceived in the US city of Boston, Massachusetts, possibly have to do with modern British beer?

When New Englander and brewer of almost three decades Dann Paquette married his partner in business and in life, Martha Simpson-Holley, in her home county of Yorkshire they were broke. After a couple of years spent living in the English countryside they grew restless and decided to return to Boston, where they originally met. Once they had relocated they decided to establish their own brewery, Pretty Things Beer and Ale Project, which launched in 2008. It would grow to become a cult favourite, forever cherished by those who were lucky enough to discover the couple's uniquely delicious beer.

Not able to afford a brewery of their own, the pair brewed itinerantly at Buzzards Bay Brewing in the city of Westport, in the far south of Massachusetts. With so little available to them in terms of resources, Dann and Martha decided to manifest their intent to brew delicious beer by creating a character who would inspire them; a living, breathing, talking grain of barley they called Jack D'Or. They gave life to him through writing, drawings and poetry. Dann would even have a dream in which the 'golden barleycorn' – as a poem of Martha's describes him – spoke to him. As well as becoming the mascot of Pretty Things, he would also lend his name to the brewery's flagship Belgian-style Saison. 'We had to summon this whole suite of beers from nothing,' Simpson-Holley tells me. '[Jack D'Or] wants beer to be made.'

Sadly, Pretty Things was not destined to last forever. In 2015 the couple got itchy feet and decided to leave their lives in Boston behind. Selling pretty much all of their possessions, including their house and their car, the couple would then spend two years travelling the world. But not before they held a leaving party in the form of a 'funeral' for Jack D'Or, a physical replica of whom even lay in state in a coffin throughout.

Having at one point considered their career in brewing to have come to its inevitable end, thankfully they would soon be bitten by the brewing bug once again. Or perhaps it was Jack D'Or encouraging them with his merry song. Either way, the pair relocated to Sheffield in 2018, establishing The Brewery of Saint Mars of the Desert in the Attercliffe industrial district to the north of the city (the name is taken from a church in the Loire region, which they visited on their travels).

The lofty reputation the couple built themselves would soon follow them across the Atlantic, with thirsty fans keen to visit their welcoming taproom and taste their incredible beers. But this wasn't the only thing to follow them across the sea. The rumoured death of Jack D'Or, it seems, was unfounded.

Dann and Martha draw their brewing inspiration from many sources, from the bright, vibrantly hoppy beers of New England to traditional 19th-century English recipes, although their greatest influence is perhaps the monastic brewing of Belgium. This is reflected deeply in the flavour and character of this charmingly golden Saison. On pouring, Jack D'Or produces a lively, white head of foam, and leads with aromas of allspice and ground coriander. Rich and full-bodied, a pronounced yet well-rounded sweetness is balanced by the white pepper spice of hops and red berry-like fruit notes called esters, produced by their house yeast during fermentation. Finally, Jack's dry finish ensures that it is as drinkable as it is complex.

While Jack D'Or's origins are relentlessly American, as a beer it is now completely of Yorkshire, bringing a taste of both new and old worlds to the insanely lucky drinkers of Sheffield. Not only does it cement the Steel City as one of the most tremendous places for beer in the UK, but it confirms Saint Mars of the Desert as one of the finest breweries anywhere in the world.

Kelham Island
Pale Rider

Location: Sheffield, South Yorkshire
Style: English Pale Ale | *ABV:* 5.2%

When trying to establish the origin points of modern British beer I battled with how far back I was going to go into the history books. The truth, I eventually realised, is that you can keep going as far back as you like, and you will continue to unearth significant beers and moments in brewing history that, somehow, conspired together to form the beer culture we enjoy today. In doing my research, one beer I felt like I absolutely couldn't leave out was Pale Rider, a beer from Sheffield's Kelham Island Brewery, which, in its day, was groundbreaking, and for my money, still is.

Established in 1990 in the beer garden of the Fat Cat pub in the Sheffield district of the same name, Kelham Island soon earned a strong reputation among the drinkers of the Steel City thanks to its characterful ales. Its founder, Dave Wickett, had bought the pub in 1981, changing its name from The Alma. Opening a pub that was dedicated to real ale was a bold move at the time for a couple of reasons: firstly, because, despite the efforts of CAMRA, the popularity of real ale was on the wane; and secondly, because at the time, Sheffield's famous steel industry was being decimated, leaving workers out of jobs and out of pocket. The knock-on effect of this meant that hospitality businesses that relied so heavily on this trade would also be hit hard by these closures.

Thanks to not only running a great pub that was loved by locals, but also to developing beers that, for the time, were considered groundbreaking, Wickett prevailed, twice expanding the brewery to larger premises nearby. And at 2004's Great British Beer Festival he picked up the prestigious Champion Beer of Britain award for a beer called Pale Rider, a strong, righteously hoppy pale that was a much-loved favourite of regulars at the Fat Cat. Remarkably, it was the first beer entered in the competition that used North American hops to take home the top prize.

Sadly, in 2012 Wickett died of cancer, aged sixty-four, having been diagnosed just a couple of years earlier. His legacy, however, still prevails in a beer that is resolutely modern, and a huge influence on much of the beer we drink and enjoy today.

My first visit to the Fat Cat in 2015 felt like something of a pilgrimage. I remember approaching the little red brick building in this now renovated part of Sheffield with a little nervousness. Not so long ago I wasn't so accustomed to drinking in unfamiliar pubs on my own (although it's an activity I have since come to relish). Crossing the threshold at just past noon, I was met with a few silent stares from the elderly couples peacefully enjoying their lunch. Who is this young interloper? And why is he taking so many photographs?

Unperturbed, I approached the bar and ordered what I had come here specifically for: a pint of Pale Rider. I remember it being a little softer and darker in colour than I had been expecting; it wasn't quite the pale-upon-pale straw tone I expect from the Golden Ales of this time. There was some malt character in the flavour too, soft and candy-floss sweet, but only fleetingly. This allowed a crescendo of hops to build with notes of candied orange peel coming to the fore, but they were restrained throughout, with a balanced, bittersweet finish forming at the end of this orchestral flourish. It's one of those first sips that I'll never forget.

Thornbridge
Jaipur

Location: Bakewell, Derbyshire
Style: American IPA | *ABV:* 5.9%

Although this book is filled with the tales of several inspirational UK beers, this is the story of perhaps the most influential of them all. When I said at the very start of this book that beer in the United Kingdom has changed forever, Thornbridge Jaipur is arguably the most likely starting point of that change.

Despite being brewed in the town of Bakewell, south of the Yorkshire–Derbyshire border, the spiritual home of Jaipur, as for all of its parent brewery's beers, is Sheffield. I confess that when I originally drafted this book I placed Jaipur in the Midlands chapter, and felt decidedly uneasy until it had been relocated. Jaipur is a beer resolutely northern in character, if not necessarily in flavour. Case in point: the effect of a session on this dangerously quaffable beer (especially when served from cask) is referred to as getting 'Jaipured' by the enthusiastic drinkers of Sheffield.

'So many people start a Sheffield crawl with a pint of cask Jaipur at the Sheffield Tap,' Rob Lovatt, who joined the team at Thornbridge in 2010 and now holds the position of production director, tells me. 'Jaipur has become synonymous with the great pub scene here.'

Jaipur's story begins in 2005, not long after Thornbridge Brewery – set amidst beautiful grounds at Thornbridge Hall – first opened its doors. The country mansion was acquired by

Thornbridge founder Jim Harrison in 2002, and on the suggestion of his friend Dave Wickett at Kelham Island, he decided to put a brewery in one of the spare buildings within the grounds. Having just picked up the Champion Beer of Britain award for Pale Rider, Wickett had hoped he'd be able to cover growing demand by brewing extra batches at the newly established Thornbridge. What he did not realise at this time was that he had set the wheels in motion for one of the most important breweries in modern British brewing history.

Two plucky, nay intrepid young brewers named Stefano Cossi and Martin Dickie were recruited to lead the brewing at Thornbridge. Dickie, better known for being one of the founders of BrewDog in Scotland, had originally applied for an assistant brewer position at Kelham Island, but was offered a job at Thornbridge with the assurance that it would allow him greater creative freedom. This sounded more appealing, so he accepted. But while the first batches brewed within the grounds at Thornbridge Hall were for Kelham Island, the summer of 2005 saw them finally release a beer of their own design.

Inspired by the emerging craft beer revolution occurring on the US West Coast, led by the likes of Stone Brewing, Pizza Port and Ballast Point, Dickie and Cossi decided to concoct an all US-hopped beer at 6%. Over a base of pale malts made from Maris Otter barley, the duo selected Ahtanum, Cascade, Chinook and Simcoe hops imported from the north-western US hop-growing region of Yakima. These imbued the beer with a bold, resinous character that carried flavours of grapefruit and mango, while giving it a citrus peel-meets-pine resin aroma. Served at a Thornbridge Hall garden party in the summer of 2005, and named after the Indian city where Harrison was married, the beer was an instant hit.

In terms of British brewing at the time, this was wildly radical. We as a nation of drinkers are fond of sessionable beers that can be drunk with regularity over a period of several hours within a fine hostelry. A beer of this strength, and voluminously hopped to boot, was running directly against the grain. But just like a classic British ale, it was incredibly drinkable – some might say ruinously so. It could be claimed this beer started a revolution within British brewing, ushering in a tsunami of North American influence that would forever change the UK's beer landscape. Not least a couple of years later when Dickie would launch his own brewery with his old school friend, James Watt, and produce a remarkably similar beer they called Punk IPA.

'What's fantastic about Jaipur is that it has become a "go to" beer. Drinkers see it on the bar and know they can rely on the quality and consistency being there,' Lovatt says. 'Its reputation means that beer drinkers know they can try the other beers we make and expect a similar level of quality. The brewing team here knows that, and what is expected of them.'

The only hardship Jaipur has encountered in its lifetime is the eternal scrutiny of its most ardent fans. Some claim that, as Thornbridge has become more successful and grown into a far larger brewing facility, the beer has changed. Perhaps it's important to recognise, however, that while in 2005 the American West Coast IPA was a relatively unknown style, today it is commonplace, and the impact it has is far less shocking to many of us. These days Jaipur is essentially the bare minimum of what is expected from a beer of this genre.

'The beer hasn't changed,' Lovatt states. "We haven't dumbed down the product to hit a price point or to appeal to more customers. I guess the only thing which has changed is that it's now in more formats, such as can and keg.'

Regardless of how you feel about Jaipur today, it's impossible to understate its impact on British brewing culture. As much as the emergence of Golden Ales like Pale Rider had their influence, so too did this wonderful beer inspire an entirely new generation of brewing talent. For me personally, there are few things finer than a gloriously conditioned pint of Jaipur on cask, especially when enjoyed in its spiritual home of Sheffield.

GREATER MANCHESTER AND THE NORTH-WEST

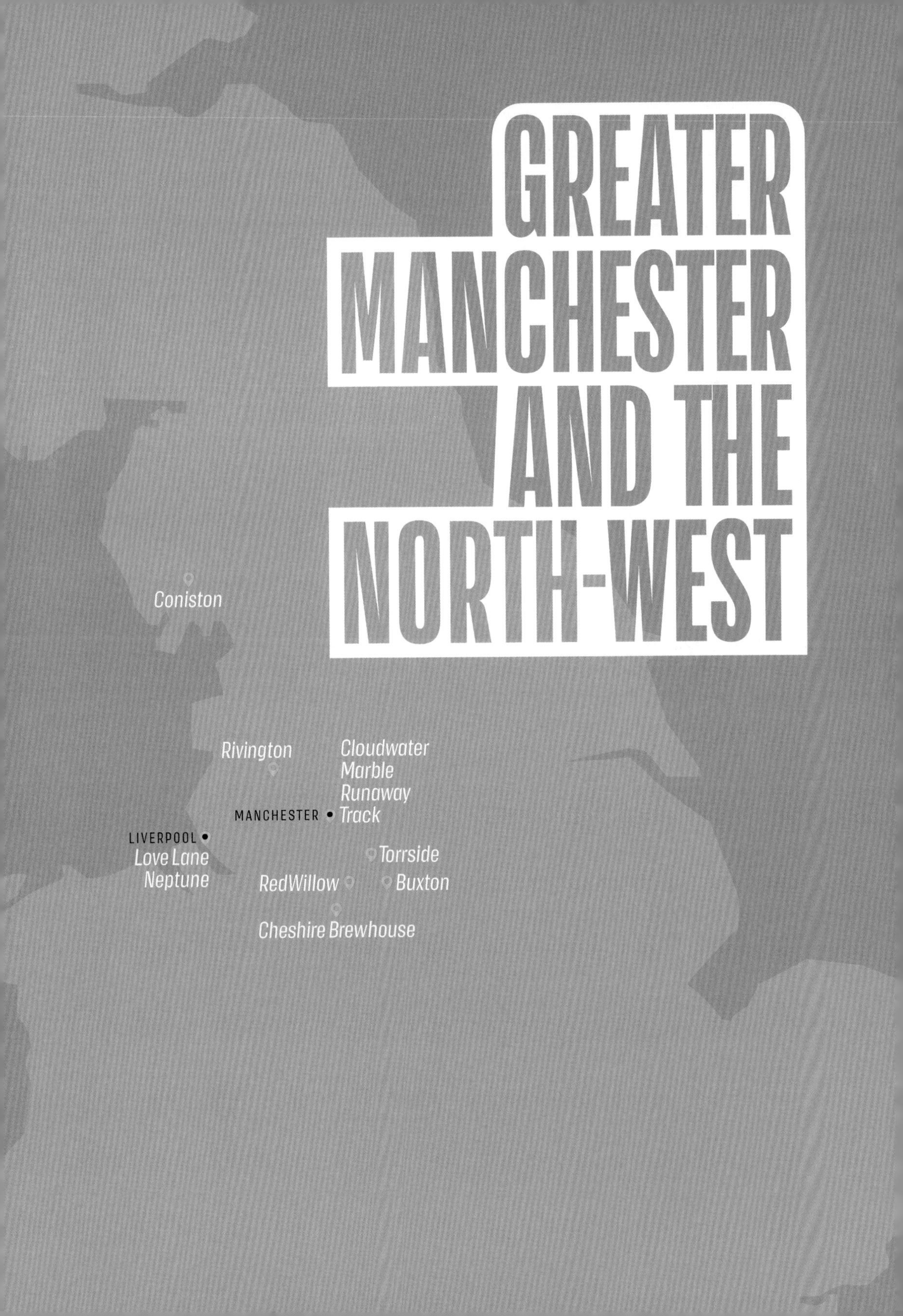

Coniston

Rivington

Cloudwater
Marble
Runaway

MANCHESTER • Track

LIVERPOOL •
Love Lane
Neptune

RedWillow

Torrside
Buxton

Cheshire Brewhouse

Manchester can be an intense place for the uninitiated. Its people are proud and defensive of its heritage, while the weather – the near constant rain in particular – is often fierce. Scratch just a little beneath the surface though, and you'll find a city that is both kind and welcoming, with any apparent haughtiness a mere facade. It just so happens that the denizens of Manchester know full well they're onto a good thing, and they're mindful to be protective of it. You can also keep the rain at bay with a decent big coat, comfortable in the knowledge that you're never far from a warm pub with a fantastically well looked after selection of ale. The latter being one of several reasons why, after fifteen years of London life, I decided to make it my home.

Step outside of the Greater Manchester area, south to Cheshire, west to Liverpool or north towards Lancashire and Cumbria, and you'll find a similar attitude in those living amidst its glorious hills and valleys, if a little more relaxed. This is a stunning part of the country, its rolling hills and forests of a particularly verdant shade of green thanks to all that extra rain. Beer – especially real ale – is cherished here and it shows in the equal care taken by those who make it, and those who cellar and serve it.

A great amount of brewing heritage is still alive in the North-West, particularly in Greater Manchester, where the family brewers J.W. Lees, Holt, Hydes and Robinsons were able to resist the encroachment of the 'big six' in the 1970s and are still going strong today. It's this reason perhaps that the pub, and in particular real ale, culture is so sturdy here. There's also a feeling within the North-West, particularly in its larger urban spaces like Liverpool or Manchester, that people like to do things their own way and not blindly follow the rest of the country. Just as this region gave birth to some of the greatest bands to have ever existed – like Echo and the Bunnymen, The Buzzcocks, Joy Division and New Order, Magazine, and Frankie Goes to Hollywood – so too has it given birth to some of the most revered breweries in the country.

From Marble, which blazed a trail from the moment it launched in the back of The Marble Arch pub in 1997, to Cloudwater, one of the most revered British breweries to have emerged in the past decade, Manchester is at the forefront of modern beer culture in the UK. It should come as no surprise that the Greater Manchester area is now home to more than eighty breweries, but this proliferation of brewing talent is not confined to one city alone. There's RedWillow in Macclesfield, Neptune in Liverpool, and Buxton, nestled in the Peak District, to name only a handful of those producing beers brimming with north-western identity and values.

Perhaps there's something in the water (coincidentally, very soft water that's perfect for brewing hoppy Pale Ales and crisp, refreshing Lagers) that spurs such a high level of creativity among its brewers. It's difficult to deny that the same energy that inspired a wealth of musical and artistic talent in this part of the country over the past few decades has now also spurred the emergence of some of the finest modern breweries in the country. They do things differently here in the North-West, and modern British beer is all the more exciting for it.

Marble
Lagonda

Location: Salford

Style: American Pale Ale | *ABV:* 5%

Jan Rogers has always done things her own way. When she was looking to boost trade at her pub, The Marble Arch, in 1997, she had two choices: invest in a karaoke machine or spend every last penny they had and put a brewery in the kitchen. I'm grateful she decided to choose the latter, as I'm sure many of you reading this are, too.

Situated on Rochdale Road, right on the edge of Manchester city centre and the creative hub known as the Northern Quarter, The Marble Arch – or just 'The Arch' to its regulars – is an institution. Its original brew kit was installed by local brewing legend Brendan Dobbin, who a few years earlier had established the now sadly defunct West Coast Brewing Company. Dobbin was already influential in that he was one of the first brewers in the UK to use the deeply aromatic North American Cascade hop. His legacy is one that modern British beer owes a tremendous debt to.

Marble's brewery is no longer located at the pub, having eventually grown out of its original space and into a railway arch not far behind it. The original brew kit found new life with the fledgling Blackjack Brewery, which opened in 2012, and the brewery, now significantly expanded from its rather humble beginnings, has found its home in Salford, on the west side of Greater Manchester.

Despite it no longer being home to any beer production, the pub still serves as a de facto Marble taproom. Merry drinkers will

flock from all over the country to relax within the warming enclave, famous for its sloping, mosaic-tiled floor. Before I decided to relocate to Manchester, The Arch would almost always be my first port of call when I visited, the twenty-minute walk from Piccadilly station perfect in length to build up a thirst for a pint that would take less than half that time to demolish. Typically, my initial selection would be Marble's popular Pale Ale, Pint, or the sensibly monikered Manchester Bitter. Thirst sated, I would move onto a glass of something a little more, shall we say, sturdy. Earl Grey IPA is always a good shout, as is the eminent Dobber (on the rare occasions it's available.)

Those are strong beers, however, and are typically best reserved until after the sun has sunk below the horizon. For daylight drinking – or any time for that matter – you want a pint of Lagonda. First brewed in 1997, not long after the brewery sprung into life, this beer was named in tribute to a car that had been lovingly restored and put back on the road by Rogers' father that same year. The 1927 2.0-litre, High Chassis Speed Model Lagonda was purchased for just £100 in 1964.

'My da resolutely refuses to make it a heritage or novelty item, no shiny brass work or changing the crash gearbox for an easier solution,' Rogers, originally from Northern Ireland and still speaking with a strong Belfast accent, tells me. 'But it still earns its keep and is used as much as possible on today's roads, including the odd competitive event and for family holidays.'

Just like the remarkably resilient family car that, almost a century after its construction, still manages to pootle around, so too has Lagonda stayed the course. Although the recipe has been tweaked and updated as palates have changed, it remains as popular as ever. At The Arch it's more or less a permanent fixture on cask and keg, and it now also features in cans, if a more portable solution is required.

Somewhat fittingly, the stewardship of this beer is now in the hands of Jan's eldest son, Joseph Ince, who took up the position of head brewer in 2017 after stints at Buxton Brewery and Huddersfield's Magic Rock. Serendipitously, Ince took over from one James Kemp (now head of beer development at BrewDog) who also trained him as a brewer during their time together at Buxton. Although Marble's beer range is never one you could have called 'traditional', the post-2010 brewery boom – which was particularly significant in Manchester – saw the brewery's recipes in need of an update. Thanks to the foresight and hard work of Kemp and Ince, they have ensured Marble's beers have remained resolutely contemporary.

'Lagonda has changed slightly and evolved slightly over the years, however we've worked really hard to make sure it kept its identity and held onto the values that made it so special,' Ince says. 'When it was first brewed it was one of the most hop forward beers brewed in the UK. I think the friendly rivalry it shared with Jaipur kept the beer at its peak and ensured all the brewers who were entrusted with it, treated it with care and respect.'

I have drunk this wonderful beer many times since I discovered it just over a decade ago. Poignantly, my final draught beer before the winter lockdown of 2020 temporarily forced our beloved pubs to close their doors for several months was a pint of Lagonda in The Arch. Its character, while always intensely hopped, has become a touch less bitter, and slightly more aromatic as the beer's development has progressed. Its primary characteristics have remained that of grapefruit and pine with a slightly floral, almost honeysuckle-like scent. The biggest change is that, after over two decades in production, Marble no longer refers to it as an IPA; its 5% ABV sets it in more sessionable Pale Ale territory by today's standards.

It's never been the kind of beer that enthusiasts fuss over, but in terms of Manchester, and modern beer in general, it's a standard bearer. 'The car is the opposite of hype – age over novelty, the fact that things have continuity, quality and beauty, despite being old,' Rogers adds. 'The same goes for the beer, it's definitely seen recipe changes over the years, but the fact it is still selling is a reminder that not everything has to be new to be successful.'

Cloudwater
The Beauty Between Power and Dreams (Double Hopfenweisse)

Location: Ancoats, Manchester
Style: Weizen Dopplebock | ABV: 8.5%

From being a company within the beer industry where more than 50% of its staff are women, to giving time and space within its busy schedule to allow Black and LGBTQ+ owned beer brands such as Eko Brewing, Rock Leopard and Queer Brewing to brew beers at its Manchester facility, Cloudwater's agenda reaches far beyond the beer it makes.

Its ebullient founder, Paul Jones, is not a man who minces his words. And neither are they in short supply. Few other brewery owners have put their reputation on the line in the name of equity,

Paul Jones

inclusion and justice in the same way he or his brewery has over the past decade. 'Cloudwater is no longer just a brand or brewery. We're a platform,' Jones says. 'Even in the short years that we've been around we've demonstrated that you can grow to a place of prominence, trust, and influence enough so you can do things to give folk a leg up.'

When it was founded in 2014 Cloudwater operated on the basis it was producing 'Modern Seasonal Beer'. In 2021 this was joined by a new ethos it calls 'Beer with Big Ideas', further expanding on the idea that this is a brewery that's interested in far more than just putting great tasting liquid in a glass. Jones is also aware, however, that beer is something that's meant to be fun. As such he's still as passionate in ensuring his brewery produces exceptional products for people to enjoy as he is about tempering that passion into its principles. It's this combination of values that has marked them as one of the leading lights in British brewing to have emerged in the past decade.

Despite the brewery building much of its lofty reputation with a range of intensely hopped IPAs – they are a pioneer in terms of bringing the hazy, intensely juicy New England style to British shores – its approach to 'Modern Seasonal Beer' hasn't changed. This is expressed through a wide range of styles the brewery releases, from traditional English Bitters and German-inspired Lagers to a beer I feel encapsulates Cloudwater's desire to push the envelope: its Double Hopfenweisse.

'That beer style is one that we are deeply in love with,' Jones tells me. 'I think they've really stood out as being beers with massive potential to open people's eyes to high protein grists, expressive yeasts and then a massive dry hop contribution.'

Taking the basis for its inspiration from a traditional German Hefeweizen, Double Hopfenwiesse fuses this with a resolutely modern Double IPA, creating a new animal entirely. While on first impression this hybrid may come off as a little bizarre, I find it to be a wonderful expression of Cloudwater's creativity and its mastery of contemporary flavours. Taking the traditional banana and clove profile of a wheat beer, it then amps that up to its maximum before layering it with waves of herbaceous and citrusy hops. Each sip is wrapped up in a pillow of oats and malt, giving the beer a thick, almost silky texture, somehow helping its off-kilter combination of flavours to remain balanced. A nod of bitterness in the finish prevents it from ever getting out of control.

For Jones, seasonality is more than just an expression of a change in the weather, or a sense of time and place. It can be political too. For Cloudwater, brewing with the seasons means producing beers that are as expressive in their flavour as they are a time, a place, and the people who drink them.

'We always express seasonality in a really basic way. Brown ales fly down your neck in autumn, and Lagers are just incredible – well, all year round – but especially when it's warm,' Jones says. 'But we've also thought about seasonality in terms of what the kind of mood is. Reading the room, asking what consumers want and how do we offer not just the liquid and the beer element, but the overall vibe.'

Runaway
American Brown

Location: **Green Quarter, Manchester**
Style: **American Brown Ale** | *ABV:* **5.7%**

Despite their inherent deliciousness, Brown Ales simply don't get enough love from the beer-drinking proletariat. I say this from experience, and as someone who loves the style. But I also feel responsible for some of its shortcomings, my propensity to reach for Lagers and IPAs more often than not causing me to overlook Brown Ales when I happen upon them. When it came to writing about Manchester, however, I could not ignore the mighty Runaway, and in turn what I consider to be the brewery's crowning achievement: its American Brown Ale.

Back in 2014 when brewer Mark Welsby established his brewery beneath a railway arch in Manchester's Green Quarter, a short distance north from the city centre, he designed a core range of four beers that appealed to his personal tastes. It featured a Pale Ale and an IPA. Nothing shocking there, but as a marked point of difference it also included a Smoked Porter, and the aforementioned Brown Ale.

'I suppose we saw our core range as a statement of intent to some degree,' he tells me. 'As inexperienced newcomers to the industry, it certainly felt like our initial beers would define us in the minds of drinkers and that felt pretty critical. Brown Ale was hardly a populist choice – so I think even then we knew it was a bit of a risk.'

American-style Brown Ales differ from their British counterparts in that they are typically a little sweeter and far hoppier. The beauty of Runaway's version is that its influences are rooted on both sides of the Atlantic, and it showcases the best features of both. Its Britishness comes from a stiff upper lip of malt, providing a robust lick of toffee apple sweetness, while its American drawl takes shape in the form of a pronounced citrusy character, recalling pithy grapefruit, tangerine and the dankness of pine resin. The latter causes its bitterness to linger on the palate for a moment, priming you for another sip.

Although other breweries may have seen their aspirations to make this style fall by the wayside, likely due to poor sales or lack of consumer interest, thankfully Runaway has persevered. It's remarkable that in a city that loves its pale and hoppy cask ales, a Brown Ale, using voluminous amounts of North American hops and which is served chilled and from a keg, has won the hearts and minds of a hardcore group of fans. Hopefully this persists, for if we keep drinking it, Welsby tells me, Runaway will keep making it.

'In retrospect, launching with a Brown Ale was probably braver than we realised at the time, although it remains really popular with a solid core of trade customers and drinkers,' he says. 'It's a beer that people are often surprised by if they can get past its unassuming appearance and initial hesitancy about a less hyped style.'

Track
Sonoma

Location: Ancoats, Manchester
Style: Pale Ale   *ABV:* 3.8%

'A pint of Sonoma please, and a bag of Scampi Fries.'

There are few more satisfying phrases that can be uttered when occupying a barstool within a Manchester hostelry, except for perhaps 'another'. Track's effusive house Pale Ale, Sonoma, is perhaps the essence of Manchester's modern beer culture distilled into liquid form. Named after the California county that so many great breweries hail from, including greats like Russian River, Sonoma swaggers with its spritzy lemon zest and lime juice character, all wrapped up in a finish that's dry and a touch bittersweet. The salt of a well-selected snack such as the example mentioned above only serving to enhance this beer's spritzy character.

While it tastes as great supped direct from a can as it does from a glass poured from a perfectly chilled keg, this is a beer that really comes into its own when served from a cask, via hand pull, through a tight sparkler. For the uninitiated, the latter is a small plastic nozzle that, instead of pouring the beer straight from one big hole, forces it into several smaller ones. This causes the carbonation within the beer to break up, creating smaller bubbles, resulting in a pour with a smoother body and a luxuriously creamy head of foam.

Some people, mostly drinkers from the parts of England that are south of Derbyshire, detest them. They will claim that 'sparkling' a beer knocks out flavour and aroma, and is an easy way to ruin a perfectly good pint. Admittedly, after a considerable amount of research, I have deduced that there are certain ales that do not benefit from being served this way – specifically beers brewed for pubs in the south of England. But for me, most do benefit, and sparklers do not strip out hop flavours or aromas, in fact, for me they only serve to enhance them.

Sonoma is a perfect example of this. A beer that revels in the softness of a smoother pour, while losing none of its strolling-in-a-citrus-grove character. Its gentle ABV of just 3.8% also makes it accessible, and perfect if you fancy a stroll around the various pubs and bars of Manchester, taking in the odd pint as you go. It's no wonder that despite Track being a relatively young brewery, founded in 2014, it's become a staple of the city's already breathtaking beer culture.

'Whether it's on cask in our local pubs or in cans in people's hands it seems to have become a go-to beer in its style, which we're really proud of,' Track founder Sam Dyson tells me. 'To have people rate it so highly means a great deal. That's what you're looking for as a brewery, people to really like and connect with a specific beer you've made. Simple really, but so hard to do.'

RedWillow
Wreckless

Location: Macclesfield, Cheshire

Style: American Pale Ale | *ABV:* 4.8%

Before he founded RedWillow Brewery with his wife, Caroline, in their home town of Macclesfield, Toby McKenzie would make the long commute back and forth to London, where he worked as an IT consultant. Little did he know, each time he did so he would pass within metres of the warehouse that would one day house his successful family business. Nor would he have had any idea that you would be able to buy his brewery's flagship Pale Ale, Wreckless, on those very trains. Sometimes the journey can be just as important as the destination.

'I was once on the train heading down to London for a meet the brewer event and was wearing a RedWillow branded top. I was called "Mr. Wreckless" by one of the train staff,' McKenzie tells me. 'For a long time this was the beer that defined us. We won a load of awards for it and it rapidly became our biggest seller in cask and bottle.'

A modern Pale Ale in every sense of the word, Wreckless is ever-so-slightly hazy in the glass, pale gold in colour, and booming with aromas of orange, lemon and grapefruit, with North American Citra and Amarillo hops to the fore. This is a beer that effortlessly walks a tightrope between intensity and restraint; interesting enough to hold the attention of hardcore beer fans, while also being accessible to those who are used to more traditional Pale Ales, or even those who are relatively new to modern, hop-forward beer.

'This was probably the first beer that we made that had a really big (for the time) charge of hops,' McKenzie adds. 'It's hard to understand just how much the brewing world has changed for Pale Ales in the last ten years.'

While RedWillow has become a recognisable name for beer enthusiasts all over the country, there's a special pride of place held for it in the hearts of north-western drinkers. This is no more apparent than in Macclesfield itself – a fantastic beer town in its own right – especially in the brewery's own bar. Here you will find all kinds of beer drinkers – men and women, young and old – coming together to enjoy the mind-blowing array of beers RedWillow now produces, and you can guarantee that most of them will be having at least one pint of Wreckless before the evening is through.

The Cheshire Brewhouse
Gibraltar Porter

Location: **Congleton, Cheshire**
Style: **Imperial Porter** | *ABV:* **8.1%**

I'm convinced we stand on the cusp of a malt revolution in the United Kingdom. I say this safe in the knowledge that British malt is the finest in the world, prized as much by distilleries in Scotland and Japan as it is by breweries across the globe. But when it comes to modern beer, the hop too often takes centre stage. My vision is that one day in the not-too-distant future we will see drinkers effusing about malted barley, oats, wheat and rye in the same way they do about those sticky, green cones of joy.

Gibraltar Porter from The Cheshire Brewhouse is interesting in that it is an obvious expression of malt; a dark beer with a massive treacle and molasses character, a hint of smoke lurking in the background throughout. Dig deeper and there's bitter dark chocolate, anise, and maybe even the tiniest hint of soy sauce-like umami, all held at bay by a resolutely bitter and profoundly dry finish. The brewery's charismatic, outspoken founder, Shane Swindells, is never one to do things by halves, and this beer is a perfect representation of that.

'Gibraltar Porter is a recreation of a beer originally brewed by Mew Langton on the Isle of Wight in the 1890s (sadly closed since 1969), with heritage Chevalier barley,' Swindells tells me. 'Ultimately the heritage side of what we do is where I want to focus.'

Despite the age of the recipe it's based on, the bold, distinctive flavours of this beer don't feel at all out of place in today's beer world. Most interestingly, as well as using English Goldings hops, Gibraltar Porter uses malt from a long since retired barley variety known as Chevalier. Resurrected from just a handful of archived seeds in 2015 by Norfolk-based Crisp Malt, Swindells has been a champion for the variety ever since, using it as the base in several of his beers, including this Porter and a sensational-tasting heritage IPA called Govinda.

When I talk about malt, I see Chevalier's resurrection is an indicator of things to come. In decades past, when brewing became more and more industrialised, malt was prized less and less for its flavour and more for the amount of fermentable sugars brewers could extract from it. The more efficient a barley was, in terms of both its yields and efficiency, the more money could be made from selling beer made from it.

But brewers have always resisted the entropy of more commercially viable malt varieties, prizing certain malts over others for their defined, characterful flavour. This is why varieties such as Maris Otter and Golden Promise have persevered in the face of industrial agriculture, where a barley variety typically has a shelf life of only five years.

Thanks to the explosive growth of small breweries there are now people like Swindells who seek to differentiate themselves in new ways. While many have done this with hops, thankfully we also have breweries like the Cheshire Brewhouse which sees the potential in the tremendous flavour and character of barley varieties like Chevalier, Hana and Plumage Archer, to name just a few.

The emergence of heritage barley gives drinkers another way to trace the beer in their glass back to the farm on which it was grown, which will only serve to deepen their connection to beer. It's because of beers like Gibraltar Porter that we're one conversation closer to malt becoming more exciting for drinkers everywhere.

Torrside
Monsters

Location: New Mills, Derbyshire

Style: Smoked Barleywine | *ABV:* 10%

With the sheer volume of breweries now vying for our attention it is increasingly difficult for a newcomer to make its mark on the beer world. One particularly old school way of succeeding in a crowded market would be to invest in capacity, grow as big as you possibly can and absorb the competition that stands in your way. Find a brand consumers love and turn your brewery into a factory that churns this product out ad nauseum.

But what if you don't want to grow into a big brewery? What if you don't want to just endlessly turn out the same old beer again and again, but instead focus on supporting a small community of beer lovers who are as passionate about the diverse products your brewery makes as you are? This renewed focus on the hyper-local market is at the heart of modern British beer, and I'd like to think that, in an ideal world, long after this book is published, an increasing number of breweries have decided to eschew traditional routes to market, instead finding new and alternative ways of getting their beer in front of those who are thirsty for it, and doubling down on the support of loyal customers who genuinely care about their beer.

Torrside Brewing, based in the Derbyshire town of New Mills, is a perfect example of this way of thinking. Set up in 2015 by a trio of former homebrewers – Chris Clough, Peter Sidwell, and Nick Rothko-Wright – the brewery quickly won the hearts and minds of neighbourhood beer enthusiasts with their mouth-wateringly eclectic range of beer. And while Torrside does produce a selection of what could be described as 'conventional' Pale Ales and IPAs to keep the purists happy, it's through their off-kilter range of smoked beers that they've become a local cult favourite. One of its beers in particular, a smoked Barley Wine, or 'Rauchwine' if you will (playing on the German for 'smoke'), had me besotted at first sip.

'Rauchwine was one of the first entries in our "Monsters" series of smoked beers, and effectively set the tone for what came after that,' Clough explains. 'It's often the beer that catches the attention of new drinkers who may not have come across Torrside before, simply by virtue of being a fairly unusual beer style that hopefully stands out from the crowd.'

In 2018 the trio decided to take things one step further and launched a festival dedicated to smoked beers, the aptly named 'Smokefest'. This was the perfect setting to showcase beers like Monsters, which requires far less caution than its name might suggest. I find smoke to be a wonderful element within beer, enhancing both the sweetness of the malt and the snap of bitter, herbaceous hops. While it can be challenging at first, and easy to compare to flavours of, say, smoked meats or bacon-flavoured crisps, there's far more nuance and complexity than it may initially seem.

As its name suggests, Monsters amplifies these characteristics, imbuing a bold, bittersweet beer with compelling flavours of beech and oak wood leading to a bitter, almost oily finish replete with warming alcohol. This is a beer where your perseverance will be rewarded; once a convert, always a convert. Then you can move on to the versions of Monsters that have been aged in spirit barrels, or have received additions of fruit such as raspberry and cherry.

'Although more breweries appear to be venturing into smoked beers recently, it remains a polarising beer style – very much a niche within a niche,' Clough continues. 'We like to think that when the subject of UK smoked beer comes up, we'd be one of the first breweries that come to mind.'

Buxton
Imperial Black

Location: Buxton, Derbyshire
Style: Black IPA ABV: 7.5%

When I began writing about beer in early 2012, the influence of the American craft brewing revolution that first washed up on UK shores in the early 2000s was approaching fever pitch. Breweries were desperate to get their hands on the limited supplies of exciting hops like Citra from the US and Nelson Sauvin from New Zealand, with the intent being to use them in the most potently bitter and aromatic beers they could produce. And plucky, beer-loving whippersnappers like myself were eager to get our hands on them so we could post about them on our websites.

Surfacing as the tide of Americanisation rose to its peak, Buxton Brewery opened in the idyllic Derbyshire town of the same name in 2009. Initially a relatively traditional producer focused on making contemporary (for the time) real ales, they too were soon bitten by the US bug, and began to innovate as best they saw fit. The appearance of its American West Coast-inspired IPA, Axe Edge, was a game changer. This was one of the few examples of the style that really hit the nail on the head at the time it was released. It provided a huge, resinous hit of mango and pine followed by a slap in the face from citrus bitterness. But despite its strength it was so well balanced that it was incredibly easy to put away several pints in quick succession. Carnage ensued.

Around 2011, as the brewery was gaining popularity in northern cities like Leeds and Manchester, it released a curious beer called Black Rocks. Buxton's brewer at the time, James Kemp (who would later brew for Marble and Yeastie Boys, and is currently head of beer production at BrewDog), developed a beer that looked like a Stout but somehow tasted like a Pale Ale. Fans loved its befuddling character, so in his infinite wisdom, Kemp decided to take things one step further and create an even stronger, more intensely hopped version. So it came to pass that Imperial Black was born.

My first experience with Imperial Black was a memorable one. Sometime in 2012 or 2013 I was standing at the bar in a popular London beer venue and didn't have a clue what to order. Watching its patrons repeatedly and excitedly order pint after pint of a dark beer, but not knowing what it was, I gestured towards someone's pint before turning my attention back to the bartender to ask for 'one of those please'. Naturally, I thought I was getting a Stout. Imagine my shock when, on tasting the beer, I did not get a roasty, toasty, rich, dark beer as I was expecting, but instead was accosted by an explosion of pineapple, and lemon rind, pursued by a gradually building bitterness that was almost tactile, such was its intensity.

Further excited sips revealed more detail; a subtle licorice character, and perhaps just the faintest touch of dark chocolate to remind me that, yes, this was a dark beer, but it was unlike any dark beer I had tasted before. Emptying my glass swiftly, but deciding I was not yet done analysing this beer, I returned to the bar and ordered another pint. I did not realise it was 7.5%. Nor do I remember how I got home that evening. At the time, discovering Imperial Black felt like I had reached the edge of the universe in terms of what a beer could look and taste like. Little did I realise at the time that I had barely left the galaxy, albeit after briefly orbiting one of its brightest stars.

Rivington
Days of Candy

Location: Rivington, Lancashire
Style: American Pale Ale | *ABV:* 5.3%

The autumn of 2020 was a particularly awkward time for people like myself who prefer to do their drinking in pubs rather than at home. Despite the requirement to wear a face mask, constantly sanitise your hands, and scan a little barcode with your phone just so you can go inside a venue becoming de rigueur, every moment of it still felt uncomfortable. I couldn't escape the feeling that being inside a pub was a risk, while conflictingly I felt like there was no place I'd rather be. In the case of a trip to Station Hop, a local bar where I enjoyed a pint of the exceptional Days of Candy from Rivington Brewing Co, it's one I am immensely glad I decided to take.

I already knew of Rivington Brewing Co by reputation, and spotting their Days of Candy American West Coast-style Pale on tap, my deliberation over what beer to order was short-lived. On being presented with a strikingly bright, Golden Ale (via table service, at a socially safe distance) I immediately pulled the glass to my face and inhaled. The classic grapefruit and pine character that typifies this style was richly satisfying, but something about the way it was structured around an almost candy floss-esque layer of sweetness enhanced its drinkability, somehow taking it to another level entirely.

'At the time, Days of Candy reflected how we wanted to stand apart from other local breweries,' Stubbs says. 'Every time we bring it out we're reminded of how much we like it, then it seems to disappear for a little while. It's one of the few beers we haven't really altered much over the years.'

Established in 2014 by Ben Stubbs and his brother-in-law, Mick Richardson, Rivington has developed an enviable reputation among the North-West's beer aficionados. This is largely thanks to Rivington's hazier, juicier beers such as the amusingly named Never Known Fog Like It, but the skill with which it constructs other styles, like with Days of Candy, is demonstrative of the breadth of its quality. In 2019 Rivington invested in an ambitious expansion of its brewery located on their family farm, some 20 miles or so north-west of Manchester. Set among the serenity of rural Lancashire, Rivington's 'Tap Beneath the Trees' is a must-visit, and allows for on-site camping if you fancy sticking around a little longer. It's the perfect place to escape from the noise of the world, and wash away all its troubles with some exceptional beer.

The pandemic has brought a lot of things into perspective. One being not only how much spending time in a good pub does wonders for our wellbeing, but how immensely challenging these times have been for small independent breweries like Rivington. I was glad to be able to support them in that brief moment in late 2020, and as I write this in the spring of 2021 I'm starting to feel optimistic about returning, and the many pints that await me once I do. Hopefully, by the time this book is in your hands, we'll be together inside the pub once again.

Coniston
Bluebird Bitter

Location: **Coniston, Cumbria**
Style: **English Bitter** | *ABV:* **3.6%**

There are several Bitters brewed today in the UK that could be described as 'legendary'. Two that always come to mind for me personally are Timothy Taylor's Landlord and Harvey's Sussex Best. The former is characteristically representative of its Yorkshire home, with its bitterness as brisk as a breeze wrapping itself over the Dales, while Sussex Best is a touch softer perhaps, more curious tasting, and perfectly at home amidst the rolling South Downs.

There's a deep sense of romance to these beers, and in the process of putting together the list for this project I decided that they are perhaps representative of another time. If this book was called 'Traditional British Beer' they would be among my first choices, but this story is about looking forward, and not diving misty-eyed into nostalgia. But this also begs a question: what marks a heritage style such as English Best Bitter as modern? And how does a brown Bitter brewed with crystal malt and English Challenger hops fit in with the idea of modernity?

'It all started in 1994 when my father visited the Gribble Inn at Chichester,' Coniston Brewery's managing director, Ian Bradley, tells me. 'He drank the beer brewed on site and was so impressed he came home with the idea for us to brew our own beer for the Black Bull.'

Set in the picture-perfect setting of the Lake District, beside Coniston Water, from which the brewery and town in which it resides takes their name, Coniston Brewery is one that in some ways feels 'traditional' in the deepest sense of the word. And yet, when you take a pint of Bluebird Bitter to your lips, it doesn't feel like you're tasting the past. In the context of its surroundings, it feels comfortably at home in the present day.

A hit with regulars from the moment it first appeared on the bar in 1998, after picking up an armful of local awards, Bradley decided to take his flagship beer to the Great British Beer Festival. 'Dad and I went down [to London] unaware of what a massive occasion the GBBF was, only to come away with the best standard bitter award which we were amazed by,' he recalls. 'Little did we know that we had also won the main event. Coniston Bluebird Bitter: Supreme Champion Beer of Britain 1998!'

Since that day, Bradley describes his brewery as running 'at capacity', yet this is not one of the grand old British family breweries. Like many other small British breweries, without perhaps the resources of their larger competitors, Coniston have always felt like plucky outsiders – something that I feel typifies modern brewing in the UK. Despite its plaudits, the brewery has also never been known to rest on its laurels. Bradley would take home the Champion Beer of Britain award again in 2012, this time for his exceptional No. 9 Barley Wine.

Coniston's seemingly bloody-minded desire to just keep doing things their way is an attitude that resonates with me. The beers are delicious, award-winning even, so why not build on this success? Expand? Make more beer and in turn it into more money? That this brewery's focus is still just on making the best beer they can and keeping those who drink Coniston beers – whether at the Black Bull itself or further afield – happy is an attitude that resonates with what I feel modern beer culture should feel like. And Bluebird Bitter is as exceptional today as it's ever been; a gentle beer, with a touch of orange zest, a little caramel and a dusting of white pepper. Never challenging, always delicious, and actually not really that traditional tasting. As relevant today as it forever shall be, Bluebird Bitter is a beer for the ages.

'It's been an amazing ride,' Bradley adds, 'And we still love brewing.'

Neptune
On the Bounty

Location: **Maghull, Liverpool**
Style: **Tropical Stout**   *ABV:* **5.8%**

Since it was established in 2015 in Maghull, to the north of
Liverpool, Neptune Brewery has playfully embraced its nautical
nature, from the maritime-inspired names for its beers to the fact
it takes its name from the family aquarium business situated right
next door to the brewery. The beers it makes are as beautifully
crafted as they are fun in nature. A perfect example of this is its
Tropical Stout, On the Bounty, which was an instant hit when it
was introduced at the Liverpool Craft Beer Expo in 2017. This is
perhaps due to its ability to unite Stout lovers and doubters alike
with its layered, yet accessible flavours.

'We thought we'd only initially brew it as a one off for that
festival. However, customers loved it, so we continued to brew it
seasonally,' Julie O'Grady, who co-founded Neptune Brewery with
her husband, Les, recalls. 'It's not a beer that people may associate
as a "stout" as it has very subtle roasted notes without a bitter finish.
We're happy that it accommodates many palates.'

Pouring as black as the abyss itself, the amusingly named On
the Bounty is a decadent mix of dark chocolate and sticky coconut.
It's a beer that's clever in its simplicity and playfulness, making
it the perfect option to give to that person in your life who claims
they don't like beer but hasn't tried the right one yet. But this beer
isn't just a starter for ten. The elegant way in which it presents an

Julie and Les O'Grady

armada of interesting flavours will cause the mouth of even the most traditional of dark beer enthusiasts to aim skywards in delight in a ten-gun salute.

'We wanted to make a dark beer with a difference to what we'd previously been brewing, and what was currently out there,' O'Grady continues. 'As dark beer lovers, we found in the summer there weren't many available in draught or can, unless you count that particular Irish Stout! We came up with the idea of brewing a chocolate and coconut Stout. A beer that could be served colder than cask and be refreshing, but also tropical in taste.'

Love Lane
Baltic Haze

Location: Baltic Triangle, Liverpool
Style: New England IPA | *ABV:* 6.2%

Situated in the heart of Liverpool's rejuvenated Baltic Triangle, Love Lane Brewery could well be the shape of breweries to come.

Set within the striking red brick of a beautifully restored former rubber factory, this is not the somewhat ramshackle brewery taproom in a cold warehouse or railway arch that you might be used to. (Not that I think there's anything wrong with the gritty urban setting of either of those – being able to enjoy beer directly from its source is nothing to be sniffed at, wherever that may be.) Here at Love Lane, there are creature comforts such as leather seats, long wooden tables where you can share some wonderful food with friends, central heating, and a range of beers to die for that are brewed on site. In fact, you can even watch as head brewer Jack Walker brews on the shiny stainless steel kit via the humongous plexiglass window that separates the brewing facility from the bar and lounge.

What I particularly like about this venue is that its charm and warmth make it accessible to all-comers: although it says 'brewery' on the outside, this isn't a refuge only for the geeks. This attitude is also reflected in Love Lane's beers, from supp-able Pale Ales to crispy, refreshing Lagers, there's something for everyone. They've got some doozies up their sleeve to keep us enthusiasts happy, too. When it was asked by SIBA – the Society for Independent Brewers –

to create a beer to celebrate its fortieth anniversary, they developed Baltic Haze, a New England IPA that is resolutely contemporary in both flavour and appearance.

'We chose to brew a NEIPA for a few reasons: the development of unique hopping techniques, choices of expressive yeasts, high protein grains and the increasing knowledge of biotransformation during fermentation,' Walker says. 'The result has proven to be an absolute fan favourite, way outstripping other beers in our taproom. From there we have constantly developed the recipe, experimenting with new hops, yeasts and more to nail down our perfect expression of this style.'

Don't worry if any of that sounds confusing. While biotransformation is a fascinating, yet still little understood process that alters hop flavour and aroma compounds present during fermentation, all you really need to know is that it results in some remarkable flavours in your beer. In the case of Baltic Haze this means instead of the sharpness of citrus or tang of tropical fruit, it presents a rich stone-fruit character, reminiscent of overripe peach and fresh apricot. There's also a sweet character to the beer, which, when coupled with the soft, pillowy body that's tempered with just the right amount of drying acidity, prevents the beer from becoming cloying, and goads you into taking repeated sips.

If Love Lane is indeed the shape of future breweries to come, as I expect, then make mine a Baltic Haze.

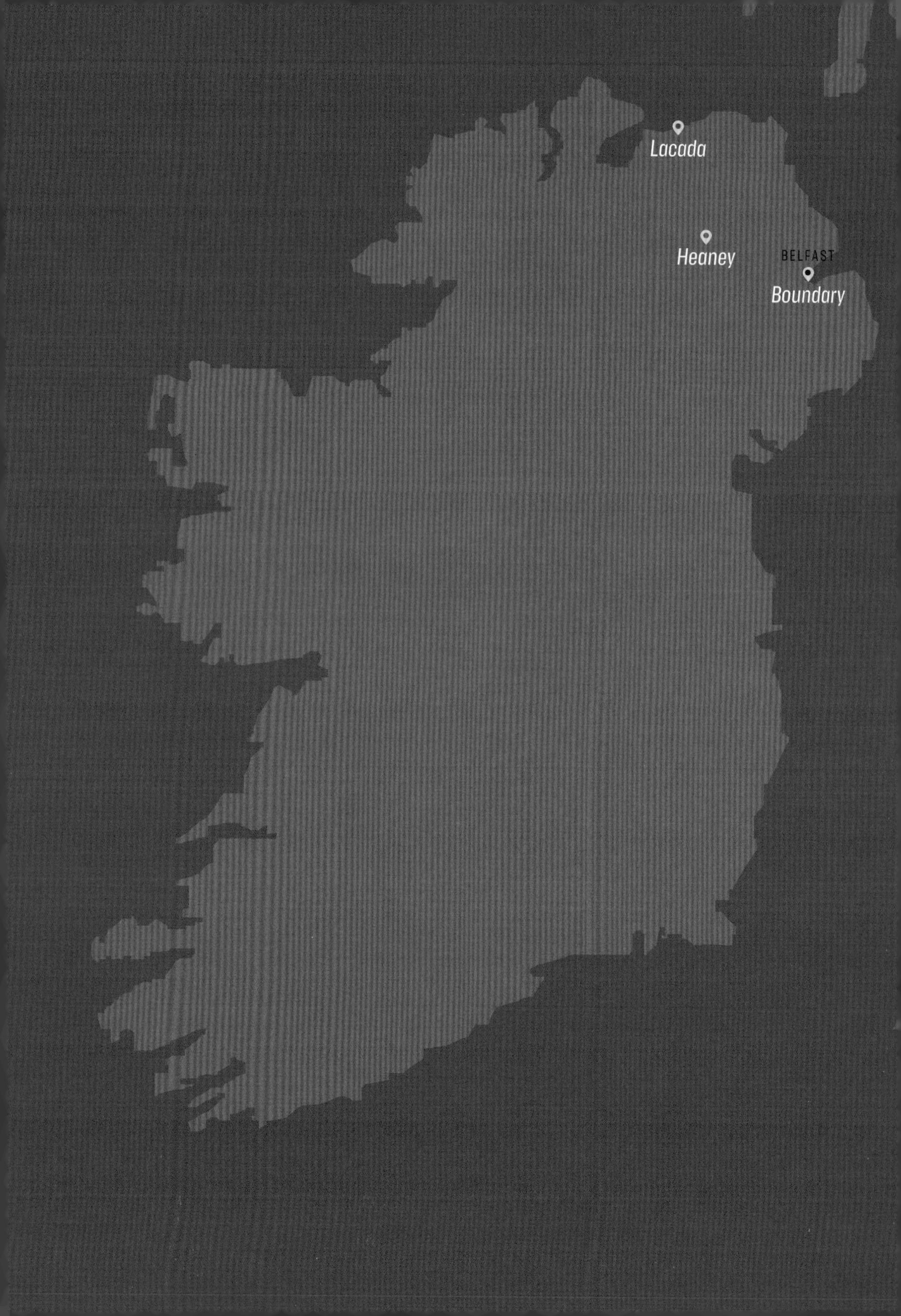

Lacada
Heaney
BELFAST
Boundary

WALES AND NORTHERN IRELAND

Wild Horse

Polly's

Geipel

Big Hand

Lines

CARDIFF

I'm aware, it's deeply sacrilegious to conflate the beer cultures of two great nations into one chapter. But the reality is that despite both Wales and Northern Ireland being home to some stupendously good breweries making outstanding beer, the scenes are more compact here. This is largely down to the fact they have smaller populations – Northern Ireland, for example, is home to fewer people than Greater Manchester. But we drinkers also shoulder some responsibility, perhaps not giving the beer of either nation the same status or credit as that of England or Scotland. For my part in this, please consider this chapter as something of a belated *mea culpa*.

Things get even more complicated when you consider that Northern Ireland is not only separated from us by the Irish Sea, but socially and culturally its beer and breweries often have stronger ties with Ireland itself, as opposed to the rest of the UK. Despite the title of this book referring to Britain, however, I felt I would be doing the incredible breweries of this country a severe injustice if I didn't find at least a little room on these pages for their wonderful beer. Northern Ireland's influence is as important to the evolution of contemporary beer in the UK as that of the other 'home' nations.

My first visit to Belfast was one of surprise and delight. Meeting with Matthew Dick, the co-founder of Boundary Brewing Cooperative, I was shown a town bursting at the seams with a vibrant food and drink culture, and I was eager to drink in every last drop. From the lively Cathedral Quarter to modern bars like Northern Lights and The Woodworkers, more traditional locals like The Sunflower, and even Michelin-starred restaurants such as Ox, Belfast's beer scene is thriving. In fact, I'd place it as one of the UK's most essential modern beer cities.

I would return several times to visit the excellent (but now sadly defunct) ABV beer festival. Taking place within the stunning setting of the Carlisle Memorial Church, this was a wonderful opportunity to experience the Northern Irish beer scene in full flow, and how passionate its people are about great beer. I hope it can return, or a similar event supersedes it, as it's the kind of event the Northern Irish beer scene deserves.

The beer scene in Wales also has a particular energy about it, much of which exists within the city of Cardiff. On its surface the Welsh capital can seem somewhat brash, its popularity for stag and hen parties and the regular march of rugby fans eager for pints perhaps unfairly colouring its deserved reputation as a city of rich culture. Scratch just a little beneath the surface, however, and you'll find a city as creative and eclectic as any other in the UK, and this extends to its beer.

But while Cardiff is arguably at the centre of the modern Welsh beer scene, there is as much regional variance between the larger towns and cities on its south coast as there is between those based in its more rural areas. Take, for example, newcomers like Wild Horse or Polly's in the north of the country, who likely find more common ground with the breweries of Manchester and Liverpool than they do with those in Swansea or Newport.

Polly's Brewing Company is a wonderful example of the progressive thinking occurring within Welsh beer culture. Among the most occult of beer circles it has quickly become one of the most fussed over breweries in the country. That they are based in the small town of Mold, a hop over the border from Chester, is also evidence of a decreasing city-centricity among modern breweries.

A shared aspect among the modern breweries to have emerged in the past decade is that they have typically been more successful if they were grounded in one of the UK's major cities. However, this is changing, with more opportunity emerging in smaller towns and rural areas as modern beer itself shifts away from urban spaces. The combined effect of overpriced property and millennials and Generation Z desperate for a slice of country life post-pandemic is now in the early stages of having a long-term effect on beer's future.

This will be hugely beneficial to countries like Northern Ireland and Wales. The relative success of breweries, including, but not limited to, Boundary and Polly's, perhaps paves the way for a new wave of brewing talent. Until that happens we can be thankful that both have positively flourishing beer scenes. Ignore them at your peril.

Boundary
Export Stout

Location: Belfast
Style: Foreign/Export Stout ｜ *ABV:* 7%

When I originally met co-founder of Boundary Brewing
Cooperative Matthew Dick in early 2016, one of the first
things I asked him was how he came up with the name for his
then fledgling business. He told me how it was a permanent
reminder that there should be a boundary between time at
work and time at home. Specifically, it comes from a quote
by French novelist, Gustave Flaubert: 'Be regular and orderly
in your life so you can be violent and original in your work.'

When Dick established Boundary in 2015 along with
business partner Matt Scrimgeour, he was looking after a
young and rapidly growing family. Having met his wife,
Sheena, when living on the West Coast of the United States
several years earlier, he returned to Belfast in 2010 and found
its beer scene considerably lacking, and saw an opportunity
for a new brewery with fresh ideas to take root. Finding the
space and capital to launch such an endeavour would elude
him for a few more years, so in the meantime he spent time
working for BrewBot, a now defunct manufacturer of an
'all in one' homebrewing solution. This afforded Dick the
time to not only hone his own brewing skills, but to speak to
breweries all over the world about some of their most cherished
recipes as he programmed them into the BrewBot system.

It was Scrimgeour who, when put in contact with Dick, suggested they look at the cooperative model – essentially launching a shareholding scheme for anyone interested in buying into the nascent Boundary. The initial offer was a roaring success, raising more than £100,000 in just eight days, in turn welcoming over 400 investors as owners of the business. Finding a suitable space in a former woollen mill in East Belfast – an area still marked with murals reflecting on Northern Ireland's troubled past – Dick brewed the first Boundary beers in May 2015.

In the years since, the brewery has established itself as one of the leading lights within the Northern Irish Beer scene, with Dick's beers showcasing a range of influences, from Belgian-tinged wild ales through to hop-accented beers guided by his years living in the US. As well as an ever-rotating range of specials, Boundary has established a core range of beers, including Imbongo, a resolutely hazy modern Pale Ale, Forever Ago, a New England-inspired IPA, and the somewhat less imaginatively named Export Stout.

The latter is a deep, mysterious and overtly delicious dark beer inspired directly by London trailblazers, The Kernel. 'I reached out to The Kernel and asked them for tips on the recipe. They shared the whole thing with me,' Dick tells me. 'It was the very first beer we brewed. And it's not really changed since.' He adds, 'It also gave me an opportunity to connect with Simpsons Malt, who we've worked with since day one. Their Brown Malt is spectacular, and is absolutely key to our Export Stout.'

The recipe is not a direct clone of the Kernel's one, more an interpretation that was tinkered with for around a year until Dick was happy enough with it to make it one of Boundary's main beers. It pours oubliette black with a rich tan head, looking almost like a freshly brewed coffee as opposed to a beer. There's no coincidence that freshly-roasted coffee is also one of its predominant flavours, but there's an intense chocolate note that makes it more mocca-chino than flat white. Importantly, it finishes dry, its drinkability belying its devilishly robust alcohol content.

Matthew Dick

It's since become the brewery's most awarded beer, but perhaps most importantly it's helped propel Boundary into the limelight, helping it usher in a huge interest in modern beer styles in Northern Ireland. Dick, who's always philosophically measured in his thinking, is concerned that modern breweries do risk looking too similar to one another, choosing the same packaging format, using the same raw ingredients, and brewing the same styles.

'I suppose that's where regionality may become even more of a USP,' he says, reflecting optimistically on the Northern Irish beer scene at large. 'Most of our customers live in Northern Ireland. They love the drinkability of our Export Stout, plus it's a better alternative to that other black shite that has decimated the industry over here.'

Heaney
Irish Pale Ale

Location: **Bellaghy, County Londonderry**
Style: **Pale Ale** | *ABV:* **5%**

Maybe this is an indicator of just how closely knit the modern Northern Irish beer scene is, but when I met founder of Heaney Farmhouse Brewery Mal McCay for the first time, it was seconds after meeting Boundary's Matthew Dick. This is no coincidence: at the time McCay was brewing at Boundary, initially picking up a few shifts after Dick broke his foot and was unable to operate the brewery. Despite these unfortunate circumstances, this was fortuitous for McCay, and for the Northern Irish beer scene in general, as under Dick's instructions he was able to learn how to brew professionally. After several years at Boundary, he would eventually open his own brewery in 2019.

The brewery is named after poet and playwright Seamus Heaney, whose father, Patrick, would have worked the land in Bellaghy, from where it draws its water. It's also on this land where Heaney's brother Hugh still farms to this day, and where the modern farmhouse brewery is based. It's by no coincidence that McCay's wife, Suzanne, happens to be a niece of the great poet himself.

His time at Boundary afforded McCay the opportunity to develop his own recipes. The brewery's core range reflects beer styles that could be considered to be classically Irish; it includes a Red Ale, a Blonde, a Stout and an Irish Pale Ale. Elegantly packaged in a slender brown glass bottle, and noticeably so amidst today's

Mal McCay

sea of aluminium, this Pale practically slinks into a glass, as you might into a cosy bar snug after a hard day's labour. Bursting with subtle notes of tropical fruit and hints of citrus, the beer first relies on a soft, yet steady malt character, almost with the air of freshly baked bread. This buoys flecks of pineapple and lemon, followed by a bitter lick of herbaceousness before this Pale Ale finishes clean as a whistle.

It's a beer that commands little attention – in the best possible way – providing the perfect means to relax into an evening and forget about the toils of the day.

Lacada
Devil's Washtub

Location: **Portrush, County Antrim**
Style: **Black IPA** | *ABV:* **5.2%**

'Devil's Washtub was a pivotal moment in the development of Lacada Brewery,' its founder and head brewer, Laurie Davies, tells me. 'We were coming up to being twelve months at market and, quite frankly, the sales weren't standing up well.'

Situated in the town of Portrush, where the Northern Irish coast meets the roaring North Atlantic Ocean, a stone's throw from the world famous Giant's Causeway, Lacada Brewery was established by Davies in 2014. The brewery takes its name from the *Liach Fada*, meaning 'The Longstone', which refers to a rocky outcrop about 300 yards east of the Causeway itself. A cooperative like Boundary, the brewery is owned by a community of shareholders, each with their own stake in the brewery, both emotional and financial.

Perhaps reminiscent of the waves that crash against the rocks of the northern shore where it resides, Lacada's first few months of existence were far from plain sailing. Its own brewers even declared the brewery's first few beers 'not good enough'. And so they decided to go back to the drawing board and invest in some better quality hops. Feeling that they'd already proved themselves with their dark beers, and inspired by a collaboration brew between Northern Ireland's Pokertree brewing and Manchester's Marble, which fused darker malts with aromatic North American hops, they decided to follow suit.

The result was Devil's Washtub, an intriguingly dark ale brewed with four types of malt and four different hop varieties. The beer is balanced in that it shows remarkable restraint for an ale of 5.2%. Hints of chocolate creep in, providing a touch of pleasing astringency, priming you for a gentle rush of pithy lemon and grapefruit, plus the slightest touch of pine resin dankness. Davies tells me that such was its remarkable hop character they originally decided to call it a 'North Coast IPA'. 'We thought it fun to be tongue in cheek,' he says. 'There's West Coast IPA, and East Coast IPA… why not a North Coast IPA?'

The beer was an instant hit, taking home a bronze at the 2017 Dublin Craft Beer Cup – the irony being that they were told if they'd entered it in the dark beer category instead of IPA it would've won gold. Chastened by this decision, they decided to drop the gimmick and relabel it as a dark ale. Later that year they'd enter it in the Taste of Ireland food and drink awards, where it beguiled the judges. Not only did it pick up five medals, it was crowned the 'best new product in Ireland' out of hundreds of finalists. The beer completely reversed the brewery's fortunes, sales grew and stabilised as the brewery built itself a fine reputation on the back of its success.

'In many respects, the Devil's Washtub is a signpost for Lacada in that we constantly want to reflect, revise and progress,' Davies says. 'Some people may have a view that co-operative businesses are unwieldy and slow to change but Lacada has proven that not to be the case.'

Lines
Vortex

Location: Usk, South Wales

Style: American Pale Ale | *ABV:* 4.4%

When it comes to modern Welsh beer, Lines Brew Co founder Tom Newman has history. His brewing journey began in his father's garage in Somerset, which in 2007 would lead him to establish The Celt Experience, a brewery that gained a fair amount of acclaim until it eventually wound down in 2016. It will be many a year before I forget the intense sensory experience provided by Brigid Fire, a smoked IPA produced by his former brewery that fused the conflicting elements of smoky umami and bitter citrus into something remarkably whole.

Thankfully, Newman's departure from Celt wasn't the end of his journey. Undeterred by its end, he established Lines the same year, giving it a home in the idyllic town of Usk, set among the rolling, forest-covered hills of Monmouthshire. The brewery takes its name from ley lines – or dragon lines as they're known colloquially – mystical pathways of energy flowing unseen beneath the Earth's surface that reputedly draw eager creatives into their path.

Regardless of how you feel about invisible lines of magical energy, it's hard to disagree that Lines' beers display a certain level of creativity. This is even reflected in their branding, with a letter and colour-coding system based on the theoretical ley lines themselves used by Newman to indicate a beers style, or the origin of its inspiration. For example, green indicates the use of fresh

fruit in a beer, while red points towards continental inspiration in beer styles such as Lager or Saison. Yellow means hops, and the sunshine-bright cans that hold the brewery's flagship 'Mountain Pale Ale' Vortex is chock full of them.

'Vortex was brewed to combine drinkability with flavour and a fresh hop bang,' Newman tells me. 'Its name reflects the centre of an energy zone in ley line law, as well as a natural spiralling process we use in the late stages of fermentation at our brewery in Usk.'

The beer itself pours a satisfying hazy shade of pale gold, and effuses aromas of apricot and tangerine. Simcoe and Amarillo hops from the American North-West provide flavours of orange zest and a touch of mango, while a 'Vermont' strain of yeast brings a touch of stone fruit acidity. Through the middle of this is a thread of spun-sugar sweetness, binding it all together in a drinkable package.

While its inspiration may lie in the realms of the unseen, Vortex is an unfussy beer, as happy accompanying a good meal as it is enjoyed on its own.

Big Hand Bastion

Location: **Wrexham, North Wales**
Style: **Welsh Bitter** | *ABV:* **4.2%**

'If we do have a brewing philosophy it would include a tenet that beers should not be a challenge to drink,' Big Hand's founder and managing director, Dave Shaw, tells me. 'I was once asked what's the best review we've ever received. It was and is: "I could stay on that all night."'

Bastion is, as Shaw explains, a simple, no-nonsense bitter, satisfyingly chestnut in colour, which fuses pale, amber and crystal malts with the hedgerow fruit and white pepper snap of English East Kent Goldings hops. These are joined by the Czech Saaz variety – more commonly found in Pilsner rather than bitter – which adds just a hint of resinous bitterness, accentuating the hop notes ever so slightly in a beer that predominantly showcases the nutty sweetness of barley malt.

Founded in the wake of being made redundant from a project manager position at Network Rail, Shaw convinced his nephew and keen homebrewer, Andy Benson, to quit his job as a secondary school teacher and join him in his new venture. Benson didn't take much convincing, and in the icy winter of 2012 Big Hand was born. Although taking their initial inspiration from the more exciting pale beers being brewed using hops from the US and other far-flung regions like Australia and New Zealand, they were an almost exclusively cask-focused brewery and decided to brew a Bitter to mark the 2014 football World Cup Finals.

Originally called 11 Knights in Brazil (a thinly veiled dig from the Welshmen in reference to the amount of time England managed to stay in the competition), Bastion has since become Big Hand's longest-running beer in continuous production. While it may not sell as well as some of their more contemporary Pale Ales, there's a certain type of customer who remains loyal to this style, and Shaw is quick to remind me that beer is brewed for everyone, without exclusion, and this includes people who've been enjoying a good pint of Bitter their whole lives.

'This market for this style is definitely smaller than for Pale Ales, but those that do yearn for a pint of "summat darker and doesn't taste like lemons" really do appreciate this beer,' he says. 'This type of customer tends to be hard to win over, but if you do manage it they are extremely loyal to that beer. They love the consistency, the security that here is a pint they liked last time and they will again.'

Geipel
Bock

Location: **Conwy, North Wales**
Style: **Bock** | ABV: **6.5%**

Geipel Brewery founder Erik Geupel (the different spelling is intentional) is the picture of a modern British brewer. In fact, his portrait should probably accompany the definition. As an American immigrant brewing German-influenced beer styles in rural North Wales, on a brewhouse of Bavarian manufacture that used to belong to a brewpub in Japan, there's little questioning how global his inspirations are. That he's channelling this into a range of beers that showcase a deep sense of place is what makes them so special.

'As a home brewer since university days I had always dreamt of starting a brewery, but I could never see a way to stand out from the crowd enough to make a valid business case,' Geupel says. 'The beer from the many small breweries in Franconia is so good it seemed to me there must be a market for similar traditional styles in the UK. I thought a local, fresh Lager would be eye-opening to UK beer lovers.'

After losing his job in the recession of 2008, Geupel took some time to travel and explore his family's German roots. It was here he learned not only that his heritage stems from the southern German regions that spawned many of the golden Lager styles that we enjoy today, but that his surname was also, on occasion, spelled 'Geipel'. This being much easier for an English-speaking person to pronounce, it became the name of his new brewing venture.

But he hit an obstacle almost immediately, finding that CAMRA's broad-brush approach to Lager had demonised this style of brewing among his target customers. That, combined with a hangover from the 1990s where the word 'Lager' was synonymous with mass-produced, bland, fizzy beers, he realised he had something of a hill to climb if he was going to convince the real ale lovers of North Wales to enjoy his slowly conditioned, bottom fermented beers.

Deciding to brew a Lager that was as different as possible to more commercial examples, he turned to the traditional Bock style. Stronger than a typical Lager and darker in colour, and pouring a satisfying shade of burnished copper, Geipel Bock marries honey-sweet malts balanced ever so slightly with a gentle finger-snap of peppery hops from the German Hersbrucker variety. There are also notes of fruit cake, almond, and even a little apricot, each adding a further layer of complexity to this beguilingly delicious beer.

Consumer opinion of Lagers, as well as CAMRA's, has changed a lot since Geipel launched in 2013. They have become increasingly popular as the understanding and appreciation of how much effort goes into proper Lager brewing has grown. Much of this has to do with the Welsh brewery's distinctively modern take on traditional German styles, each successive batch bringing a taste of Bavaria to the gently sloping hills near Snowdonia National Park that the brewery calls home.

'While it is probably too unusual to be a huge commercial success, our Bock has always been very popular with connoisseurs,' Geupel adds. 'We're very proud of it.'

Wild Horse
Off Season

Location: Llandudno, North Wales
Style: Red Ale | *ABV:* 5.3%

Just like its cousin, Brown Ale, beer towards the red end of the spectrum rarely enjoys the same limelight as its pale and golden brethren. This isn't because Red Ales don't have a strong fan base, they do, and I count myself among them, but for reasons that often escape me, they just don't have the same appeal. For the sake of those of us out here who do enjoy them, I'm asking you to please give Red Ales a chance. There's something immensely satisfying about receiving a sparkling glass of crimson-tinged beer, topped with a just off-white head of tightly packed foam, an aroma of fruit cake, citrus and freshly-baked rye bread tempting you in for that first yawning gulp.

This is how I feel about Off Season, a tantalizing Red Ale from Wild Horse, a brewery based in the seaside resort town of Llandudno on the north coast of Wales. The origins of this beer go right back to when the brewery was established in 2015. Even as recently as then, modern beer looked a little different to how it does now. This was a time when hoppy beers were becoming ever more popular, but the softer, hazier iterations of IPA that emerged in the north-east of the United States hadn't yet become the phenomenon they are today. When they launched, Wild Horse had the confidence to produce beers in a range of colours and styles, not immediately leaning heavily into pale and hazy beers as the industry's most recent newcomers now tend to.

'North Wales is a big inspiration for our beers and there are really defined seasons as well as seasonality in terms of the tourist season, especially here in Llandudno,' Dave Faragher, who founded Wild Horse with his wife, Emma, tells me. 'The name comes from how quiet Llandudno gets after the mad summer season. We feel that American Red Ales are a perfect fit for the Autumn and the change in temperature and weather that comes with it.'

Off Season is a beautiful, albeit slightly more crimson-hued reflection of classic West Coast American IPAs; all dank pine and oily citrus, bound by a ribbon of barley malt. The addition of rye to this beer's grain bill adds hints of white pepper spice and a note almost reminiscent of caraway seed. Coincidentally, it also has a sister beer, fittingly called No Vacancies, which is a Pilsner brewed in the summer months when the town is packed with tourists. Despite being something of a sun worshipper myself, however, I'll still count down the days and weeks to autumn, and a time when I can revel in delectable Red Ales like Off Season once again.

Polly's
Rosa

Location: Mold, North Wales

Style: New England Double IPA ⎸ *ABV:* 8.5%

Like it or not, now is the time of the Hazy IPA. These kinds of beers feature heavily within the pages of this book and, in terms of style, it is surely one of the biggest signifiers of modern beer as we head into the roaring 2020s. The style originated from innovators in the north-eastern US states of Vermont, Maine and Massachusetts – hence it is typically referred to as New England IPA. Here, breweries such as The Alchemist, Maine Beer Co and Trillium were focused on trying to produce the softest, juiciest beers they could, perhaps spurred on by the development of newer, more intensely aromatic hop varieties such as Mosaic, as well as developments in dry-hopping, where hops are added during fermentation rather than boiling. Now, in terms of modern beer, the style has become a global phenomenon.

Generally speaking, while boiling hops creates bitterness, the process of dry-hopping imparts aroma, while also binding with yeast and proteins in suspension, giving these beers their naturally hazy appearance. Seeking to capitalise on this haziness, breweries also tried to make the mouthfeel of these beers as soft and pillowy as they could, using even more protein-rich grains such as wheat and oats to further intensify the character of these beers.

Evolution in beer is often marked by resistance, and perhaps these beers emerged as a retort to the intensely bitter, resinous beers that had become popular on the American West Coast. Or perhaps there's another reason. It just might be that clever brewers realised that not everyone actually likes bitterness, and by creating beers that are softer, and lean towards approachable flavours of tropical and stone fruit they could win over an entirely new generation of drinkers. If modern beer is to be successful, then it must become increasingly accessible, and there is no arguing that the emergence of the Hazy IPA turned an entirely new wave of drinkers onto beer.

Following the emergence of these styles in the US, a wave of innovative breweries in the UK attempted to recreate them, with varying levels of success. Notably, Manchester's Cloudwater pioneered the hazier end of the spectrum with its DIPA series, as did breweries like Verdant in Cornwall, Deya in Cheltenham, and Brew by Numbers in London.

Another brewery that has made this style its own is Polly's. Established in the Welsh town of Mold, not far from the English border and the city of Chester, it has wowed fans with its mastery over hazy, and potently hoppy IPA since its launch in 2018. Although the brewery creates countless beers in this style at various strengths, its Double IPA Rosa might just be the jewel within its crown.

'I think Rosa is where we're at our most comfortable as a brewery,' Arron Fellows, Polly's head of sales, tells me. 'We've always subscribed to the idea that we would never take on a style of beer that we don't have the utmost confidence we can do well and wouldn't drink ourselves. We'd rather be really, really good at a few styles than just okay at loads.'

Rosa is a wonderful example of a modern IPA in the New England Style. Opaquely yellow in the glass, its aroma booms with the scent of peach, apricot and mango. The mouthfeel is character-istically soft and slick with a veritable fruit cocktail of flavours, a delicate acidity keeping it all in check, preventing it from ever becoming overly sweet or cloying. Its bitterness is just a whisper amidst the haze, with its judicious hopping masking all traces of its lofty 8.5% alcohol.

'Releasing Rosa back in 2019 certainly gave us the confidence that these big, bombastic beers had a place in our output,' Fellows adds. 'It's built our reputation to where we are today – producing beer out of a brewery eight times the size of the humble little stable where we brewed our first beers.'

POLLY'S
Double India Pale Ale
'Rosa'

THE MIDLANDS AND EAST ANGLIA

Titanic

Salopian

NOTTINGHAM
Neon Raptor
Black Iris

Brewsters

Duration

NORWICH
Grain

Oakham

BIRMINGHAM
Dig

Braybrooke

Purity

CAMBRIDGE

Burnt Mill

Little Earth Project

Throughout my life I've always found the stretch of country we call the Midlands incredibly hard to define; its borders are amorphous, shifting depending on who you ask. Originally hailing from North Lincolnshire myself, I've often been told that I am of the Midlands, and yet have never identified with it. When I went to university in the North-East I was referred to as a southerner. And when I made my home in London, I was a northerner – at least until my accent eventually softened, and like most people who live in the capital for a long time, was adopted as one of its own.

None of this is to say that the Midlands lacks identity, because it has it in spades. These lands are full of character: from England's second city, Birmingham, and the Black Country to the flatlands of East Anglia, the beautiful scenery of the Shropshire Hills and back across the country again to Nottinghamshire and my birthplace of Lincolnshire; its people dogged, dynamic and creative. Yet, due to the eternal culture wars between the North and the South, it can often get a little lost amidst all the shouting, and, more often than not, I feel this also applies to its beer.

My experience of the North and of the South is that people take pride in their beer culture to the point where it becomes a great desire to tell as many people about it as possible. In the Midlands, however, I've always found the scene to be a little more guarded.

There's a deep awareness of how good the beer is here, but its people don't seem to feel the same need to tell absolutely everyone about it. Call it modesty. They'll tell you the beer is good, not great, but they'll also expect you to put the effort in to visit and find out exactly how good for yourself. And you should.

I feel like this attitude has long existed in the Midlands. Take, for example, one of its oldest family owned breweries, Batham's, which has been brewing in the town of Brierley Hill, to the west of the Birmingham metropolitan area, since 1877. While not the picture of what you'd call modernity, its significance is that those who know how good it is are deeply fanatical about the beers it produces. But they'll let you know this with a knowing smile, rather than excitedly posting about it on social media. You'll find the same reasoning when it comes to the breweries that span the worlds of modern and traditional, from Salopian in Shewsbury, to Brewsters in Grantham, and Purity in Alcester.

Despite appearing to have a more sheltered outlook on its exterior, some of the most exciting new breweries in the country are also taking root here. Birmingham is experiencing a modern beer renaissance with breweries such as Dig, Glasshouse and Green Duck; Nottingham, too, with the likes of Black Iris and Neon Raptor. And in the wilds of Norfolk, a fledgling Duration Brewing has established a blueprint for a new kind of modern rural brewing. The latter is something I predict we'll see a lot more of as Millennials and Generation Z grow increasingly tired of city life, perhaps exacerbated by months under stressful lockdown due to the Coronavirus pandemic.

The future of modern beer in the Midlands is incredibly exciting. But we still need to figure out where its borders lie, at least in terms of its beer culture. A cursory glance behind the bar to see if the sparklers are still attached to the hand pulls is often a clue (but not a given). Perhaps it's time for the passionate folks involved in the beer scene here to be as vocal as those outside of it, as this part of the UK is one all lovers of beer should be paying close attention to.

Titanic
Plum Porter

Location: **Stoke-on-Trent, Staffordshire**
Style: **Porter** | ABV: **4.9%**

There is no other beer that says 'It's Christmas' to me like
Titanic Plum Porter. It's a glass of pure opulence, superb straight
from a bottle, but really coming into its own when served with a
luxuriously creamy head via the medium of cask (through a tight
sparkler). Pouring a vividly satisfying tone of ruby red, glowing
in a way that's almost opalescent when held up to the light,
Plum Porter seduces with aromas of stewed plums and rhubarb
crumble, drawing you in for that first, decadent sip. And while
on its surface this is a relatively traditional Porter, fusing Maris
Otter with dark crystal malt (which produces its divine colour),
it's the signature note of rich stone fruit that gives it such a warm
and reassuring character. A sprinkle of peppery hops in the finish
ensures that its relative sweetness never becomes overbearing.

In 1988, three years after it was founded, Titanic Brewery was
close to sinking into the briny depths just like its namesake when
it was saved from receivership by brothers Keith and David Bott.
Over the past three decades the Botts have transformed Titanic
into a brewery that Stoke-on-Trent can be proud of. They now own
nine pubs in the area, serving a range of styles from traditional
Bitters and Milds right through to modern Pale Ales and IPAs.

But it's Plum Porter, released somewhat boldly in 2011 when
beer drinkers enthusiasm for dark beers was at an all-time low,

that has since become is best-selling and most awarded beer. Despite how well it pairs with a crisp, winter's evening, it's a beer that will provide comfort no matter what the season. It's one of those rare beers that, if you happen to see its pump clip gracing the hand pulls, you can't help but order yourself a pint – or two. Plum Porter serves as a permanent reminder that we should never restrict our fondness for darker beers only to colder seasons.

Salopian
Darwin's Origin

Location: Shrewsbury, Shropshire
Style: English Bitter | ABV: 4.3%

Situated in the village of Hadnall, just five miles north of Shrewsbury, and surrounded by the gently rolling green fields of Shropshire, Salopian Brewery has been quietly producing beers of supreme quality since it was established in 1995. The brewery is perhaps most cherished among keen beer enthusiasts for what it calls its 'Black Range': beers such as the powerfully hopped Kashmir IPA and the delectable Polygraph Imperial Stout. Locally, however, they're also highly thought of for producing some exceptional cask ales. While some, such as Oracle and Lemon Dream, lean towards a modern, citrus-forward hop profile, others nod towards the very best elements of traditional British beer.

Darwin's Origin is one such example. Copper in colour, on first sip it's a celebration of malted barley; spun sugar with a little almond noodling around in the background. That's about as traditional as this beer ever gets though, as a blend of Centennial and Mosaic hops from the US add notes of freshly zested lemon, a touch of pineapple, and an ever-so delicate honeysuckle aroma. It's a perfect example of how this brewery is able to reflect on its traditional roots while also looking forwards.

'At around the time we first brewed the beer we were shifting our focus from brewing a Midlands-style low hopped cask beer to a more modern hop forward style, for which we are now renowned,'

Wilf Nelson, who's been chair of Salopian Brewery since his appointment in 1998, tells me. 'Darwin's Origin perfectly reflects the ethos of our production, except that it is probably the only product we brew that tries to encompass a traditional style in Best Bitter.'

The beer was named in honour of Charles Darwin, a Salopian himself. The beer was first brewed to celebrate the bicentenary of the famed naturalist's birth in 2009. It's an aptly named beer too, not just because it celebrates one of the county's best-known sons or daughters, but that, as a beer, it's a beautiful reflection of the evolution of one of British beer's most revered classic styles, one that, thanks to its melding of old and new, will be appreciated by drinkers for a long time to come.

'I think it's appreciated because it's a little unusual in concept,' Nelson adds. 'And that people like to be able to identify with its heritage.'

Dig
Fazers on Stun

Location: **Digbeth, Birmingham**
Style: **Saison** | *ABV:* **6.8%**

Birmingham is fast becoming one of the most exciting beer cities in the United Kingdom. Of course, locals will tell you that the scene has always been good here, from great pubs serving exceptional pints of cask ale to modern craft beer bars keeping their taps up to date with cutting-edge beers.

More recently though, the city has been experiencing something of a renaissance in this respect. Granted, this is an outsider's perspective. But from my point of view Birmingham has recently kicked things up a notch in terms of its modern beer, with a new wave of breweries bringing with them a breath of fresh air and armfuls of hoppy goodness. One of these is Dig Brew Co. Based in the suburb of Digbeth, on the eastern edge of the city centre, the once-industrial area is becoming a hive of street-food markets, artist collectives, and breweries like Dig.

Fazers on Stun is a prime example of Birmingham's food and drink revival in action. Alongside a Double IPA known as Waka/Jawaka, it's one half of a pair of beers produced in collaboration with chef Brad Carter, proprietor of the Michelin-starred restaurant Carters of Moseley. What sets these beers apart from others in their style is that they only use British ingredients – something that Carter is also passionate about with the compelling dishes he creates. In order to conjure the modern flavour profile today's beer enthusiasts expect from a DIPA, Waka/Jawaka uses the latest developments in British hop breeding, including the Jester, Harlequin, Olicana and Opus varieties that give the beer a flavour somewhere between fresh strawberry and ripe stone fruit.

Fazers takes this concept even further, however, going as far as using foraged pineapple weed alongside these new British hop varieties, which (unsurprisingly) imbues the Saison-style beer with zingy, tropical fruit notes that mingle with peach and apricot, before finishing dry as a bone. The combination of these qualities ensures that it pairs exceptionally well with food. But it's more than capable of holding its own without an edible accompaniment, should you desire.

'We see our route to improving as a brewery and as individual brewers and makers as being one of repetition and controlled experimentation,' Dig's founder, Oliver Webb, tells me. 'With Waka/Jawaka we found some ingredients no one seemed to be interested in, while Fazers was our NASA space beer programme: "be brave let's go for it".'

Purity
Pure UBU

Location: Alcester, Warwickshire
Style: English Bitter   *ABV:* 4.5%

The first thing that hits you on the approach to Upper Spernall Farm, home of the award-winning Purity Brewing Co, is the smell. It would be obvious to blame this on the herd of Longhorn cattle that lives here, and also lends its name and image to one of this brewery's beers. However, closer inspection will lead you to a series of man-made ponds that form what's known as a reed bed system. Through it, Purity sustainably filters its wastewater until it's ready to be safely returned to the wild. From then on it can once again be utilised to make yet more pints of delicious beer.

Pure UBU is a traditionally minded beer from a forward-thinking brewery, one that is as committed to minimising its impact on its rural environment as it is on ensuring the beers that leave its facility are of the highest quality. The Best Bitter featured as part of their line-up when the brewery launched in 2005, alongside a Golden Ale aptly known as Pure Gold, and both are mainstays of its production to this day. The beer takes its name from a now sadly departed canine friend, Tess, who, in her senior years on the farm, was more commonly referred to as a 'useless bloody urchin'. Her likeness still appears on the pump clip to this day.

'Great beer with real character is what we are all about at Purity and since 2005 Pure UBU envisages all of this,' Purity's Paul Brazier tells me. 'Pure UBU has become synonymous with

Purity to the point where people often refer to us as the UBU brewery.'

While its roots are tied to the glorious history of English Bitter through its use of crystal and black malts – imbuing the beer with an inviting amber colour and a malt character reminiscent of crushed digestive biscuits – its hop selection adds a modern twist. North American Cascade adds bittersweet citrus with a fulsome grapefruit zest quality, molding your face to a semi-permanent pucker, primed for repeated sips. While Purity has never been subject to the hyperbole that exists in beer's inner sanctum, it's been proudly and contently brewing beer that's as loved in the pubs of the Midlands as it is in some of the top restaurants in London and beyond. That it's as committed to its sustainability as it is to the great beer it produces makes it as current as any other in today's beer industry.

'As the market and beer environment has changed, one thing has remained for us is quality,' Brazier adds. 'Pure UBU is probably the real testament of quality at Purity.'

Braybrooke Keller Lager

Location: Market Harborough, Leicestershire
Style: Kellerbier | *ABV:* 4.8%

The foundation of British beer, be it modern or traditional, is real ale. Speak to anyone who is passionate about beer from outside of the UK, and they will tell you how much they love drinking cask beer. Other countries have even tried to imitate it – you can find cask ale across the US, and even in Belgium! None, though, have managed to replicate the blissful quality it possesses when expertly cellared, conditioned and served in a traditional British pub setting. It's what makes British beer stand out on a global scale.

However, when it comes to modern British beer, Lager, the cold fermented, golden and refreshing beer style that emerged from the Bohemian and Bavarian regions of Central Europe in the 19th century, has just as much skin in the game. I'm not talking about mass-produced, commodity Euro Lager that's artificially (and heavily) gassed and served at a highly margin-sensitive price point. No, I'm talking about proper, traditional Lagers like the Germans and Czechs have always made, and which, over the past decade, has seen a resurgence among the UK's small breweries that are now making some the finest examples of the style.

There's a reason why Lager has grown to become the most popular kind of beer the world over, and that's because it's as delicious as it is refreshing. Beers like this outstanding Franconian-style

Kellerbier from Market Harborough's Braybrooke Beer Co are reminding us just how good Lager can be.

'As a style I feel Kellerbier captures perfectly the moreish drinkability of fresh cask ale, with an added thirst quenching quality from it being a Lager,' one of the brewery's founders, Nick Trower, tells me. 'It also works amazingly with the delicious pork knuckle and dumplings served in the Bamberg brewpubs. We have a drive to create a beer that works as well on its own as it does as an accompaniment to food.'

In order to ensure his Lager was as authentic as possible when establishing Braybrooke, Trower teamed up with Stephen Michel, the fourth-generation owner of Bamberg's revered Mahrs Bräu, and hired experienced Lager brewer Mario Canastrelli. They installed a brewery that could perform the necessary decoction mashing (as opposed to the traditional British method of infusion mashing), horizontal lagering tanks with which to mature the beer for extended periods of time at temperatures just above freezing, and even installed a reverse osmosis system that would allow them to accurately recreate the soft-water profile of Franconia. The brewery even sources its ingredients from Germany; hops from Tettnang and malt from Bamberg.

Braybrooke specialises in Lager only, and Keller Lager is proudly its flagship, providing a delicate herbaceous snap of noble hops as the high notes to accompany a deep, rounded bass section of soft, almost chewy malts. Delicate, naturally formed carbonation is almost cask-like in its softness, allowing all the flavours to resonate in a delicious, easy drinking beer.

'Lager doesn't have to be a bland, fizzy drink and we think it should be revered as an equal to ale,' Trower says. 'By looking to make our Lager in the most authentic and delicious way we can we would like to think we have ended being a modern British brewery with some very traditional values.'

Neon Raptor
Centaur Army

Location: Nottingham

Style: Imperial Stout | *ABV:* 13%

Memory is a powerful thing, especially when it comes to flavour. There are certain tastes from my childhood that have a calming, almost restorative quality to them. Call this something of a confession, but for me there is no crisis that a carton of McDonald's chicken nuggets dunked in those little tubs of barbeque sauce can't – at least temporarily – solve.

This realisation of how certain flavours carry a reassuring element to them occurred to me when thinking about the rise in popularity of much sweeter, and far less bitter types of beer that have emerged over the past five-or-so years. At the time of writing this book, two of the most fawned-over styles by hardcore beer enthusiasts are New England IPAs and so-called Pastry Stouts, the latter designed to imbue tremendously strong dark beers with flavours straight from the confectioner's counter. Both styles are remarkable in the fact that they eschew bitterness – which for me personally has long since been the hallmark of a competently made beer. But the sudden rise to prominence of these newer styles, particularly among people who are relatively new to beer, potentially indicates that expanding the scope of flavours available to drinkers has the power to bring even more people into the culture of beer – some who previously might not have given it a second thought.

The beer rating app and website Untappd provides some insight into this. If you dial into the top fifty rated beers in England it's almost entirely populated by NEIPAs and Pastry Stouts. Sitting at number three in the table overall (even when including every style of beer made in the UK) is Centaur Army, a 13% peanut butter, chocolate and caramel Imperial Stout from cult Nottingham favourites Neon Raptor. It's a beer that plays into the fact that modern breweries don't just have customers, they have fans, and that in today's market creating strong engagement with them is every bit as important as producing great tasting beer.

'Centaur Army was first conceived of in late 2019 via our followers on Facebook,' Neon Raptor's Tom Ainsley tells me. 'We asked the world of social media what they would like our 100th batch to be, giving them a few options. They unanimously chose an Imperial Stout.'

The input from their ardent followers didn't stop there. When asked what flavours they'd like to see from the beer, 'peanut butter was overwhelmingly the winner,' according to Ainsley, with caramel and chocolate also far ahead of any other suggestions. With the poll complete, the beer's concept was simple: they were to recreate an alcoholic Snickers bar. And yes, peanut is indeed the most overwhelming aroma in this infinitely black beer. Even its head has a rich, dark caramel ochre. To taste, it's intensely sweet, like crème caramel and panna cotta served alongside a double espresso, but with none of the astringency of the latter. It's pure childhood nostalgia in a can, and I am unsurprised that it is so popular with those who are less keen on more traditional styles of beer.

'We'd like to be recognised as a modern brewery that understands traditional methods enough to be able to play around with them,' Ainsley says. 'There are a lot of drinkers out there that aren't interested in a perfectly kept pint of cask Bitter or a Czech Pilsner.'

NEONRAPTOR
Brewing Co.

CENTAUR ARMY
PEANUT BUTTER, CHOCOLATE AND
CARAMEL IMPERIAL STOUT   13%

Black Iris
Rise & Shine

Location: Nottingham
Style: Coffee Stout | *ABV:* 5.2%

How do you take your coffee in the morning? Straight up, black? White and two sugars? How about in a delectably vigorous Coffee Stout brewed by one of Nottingham's finest breweries, Black Iris. While I'm not advocating that you select a beer as your morning beverage of choice (unless it's a particularly indulgent weekend) I can't recommend enough the galvanizing character of Rise & Shine Coffee Stout. It doesn't use any old coffee either, with the brewery working with locally based roaster Outpost to dial in exactly the right flavours in each batch.

'This beer was forged out of friendship and local collaboration,' Black Iris' head brewer, Alex Wilson, tells me. 'Rise & Shine is one of the few beers in our range that we produce for all our packaging formats, which proves just as popular with the real ale cask crowd as it does with the can focused craft crowd.'

The relationship with Outpost began when Black Iris relocated from The Flowerpot pub in Derby, where Wilson had been brewing itinerantly, to their permanent home in Nottingham. Any brewer will tell you that making a lot of good beer demands a lot of good coffee, and coffee can have flavours just as varied and complex as hops or barley, from red wine to stone fruit, chocolate and even lemon zest. In fact, the process of roasting the darker grains that are used for making styles such as Stout and Porter is remarkably similar to the way that coffee is processed. Although they've experimented with different coffees from batch to batch, today the brewery uses Outpost's Timber Town Espresso Blend, a 50/50 blend of Ethiopian and Peruvian arabica coffee beans.

Even as a standalone Stout, Rise & Shine would be highly enjoyable; dry and roasty, with coffee notes of its own from the malt. The addition of coffee beans twice in the brewing process – once in the boil to add bitterness, and again in cold conditioning for aromatics – imbues the beer with the honey, hazelnut and chocolate characteristics. There's a subtle yet satisfying astringency to it, adding a moreishness and accentuating those chocolate notes. I like it best on cask, but it works brilliantly in any format.

'This beer is one that our customers keep on coming back to time and time again,' Wilson says. 'The local link to Outpost means people can support two businesses at once and that means a lot to locals. Nottingham is such a fantastic, vibrant city, which we love to celebrate at any opportunity.'

Brewsters
Aromantica

Location: Grantham, Lincolnshire
Style: Golden Ale | *ABV*: 4.2%

Part of me is disappointed that Lincolnshire hasn't seen the same evolution in terms of its beer as other parts of the country. I was born in, and raised just outside of Lincoln itself, but despite it being home to a few decent pubs, it is not what I would describe as a beer town. I fear it may never be, but there is always hope.

This is not to say that Lincolnshire is not home to some truly excellent breweries, and one such example is Brewsters, based in the market town of Grantham. Founded by brewer – or should I say brewster – Sara Barton in 1998, it's been wowing the palates of East Anglian drinkers ever since. The brewery's name harks back to the brewsters of old; the women at the centre of pre-industrialised communities who were responsible for, among other things, making beer. As well as being a reference to this history, the name is also a nod to the fact that when Barton entered the industry in 1989, after receiving her master's degree in brewing and distilling from Heriot-Watt University, she was entering a male-dominated industry. Largely, and disappointingly, this is still the case. Although thanks to the pioneering work of trailblazers like Barton, it is considerably less so. Brewster's is a brewery for Lincolnshire to be proud of.

Aromatica, the brewery's Amber Ale hopped with North American Citra, is a perfect example of Barton's forward-thinking approach to beer. Originally brewed to enter into a local beer competition, it hums with notes of passion fruit and lime, but as a point of a difference its use of amber malt adds just a slight nutty character, a little reminiscent of almond and hazelnut. In a local beer competition run by the Society of Independent Brewers (SIBA), it took gold, before then taking silver in the same category in the national competition.

'We are well known for our classic style hoppy but well balanced golden brews and we like to experiment with new varieties,' Barton tells me. 'I think it is complex with its blend of multiple hop varieties to give a multi-dimensional hop flavour in a very drinkable beer.'

Oakham
Jeffrey Hudson Bitter (JHB)

Location: Peterborough, Cambridgeshire
Style: English Bitter | *ABV:* 3.8%

'This beer doesn't taste as good as it used to.'

Speak to anyone who's been obsessive about beer for a long time and they will tell you about a former favourite of theirs that has changed, irrevocably. The beer in question may be muted where its flavour used to sing, or now lacks a certain quality or character that it formerly possessed, causing it to sink in expectations and join the ranks of supposedly lesser beers.

Beer recipes change all the time, of course, sometimes in the space of a single batch. I think it's important to remind ourselves that beer is something that's grown in the ground. The very nature of it being an agricultural product means that two of its four ingredients, hops and barley, will yield in varying volumes, quality, and even flavours from year to year. While the latter is less of an issue for barley, when it comes to hops, a variety can taste remarkably different from one year to the next. How well the hop flowers – and the various oils and acids within that contribute towards a beer's flavour, aroma and bitterness – develop from year to year depends on the amount of sunlight it gets, or the amount of rainfall it receives. Hops will also change in taste depending on where in the world they are grown. This is similar to what in wine is called *terroir,* meaning 'of the earth', and is used to describe how a wine's inherent flavour reflects its sense of place.

Alex Kean
head brewer at
Oakham Ales

Beer has terroir too, but not in the same way as something as closely connected to agriculture like wine or cider. In beer, ingredients are flown in from all over the world, and in the case of yeast, cultivated in laboratories. But that doesn't mean a brewery can't imbue its own sense of place into the beers it creates. It's for this reason I believe that building a stronger connection between a drink and its agriculture is important.

While the flavour of a particular beer is influenced by the growing conditions of its ingredients from year to year, it's a brewer's role to ensure that these changes are barely perceptible. One's perception of what makes for an 'improvement' is debatable though. And let's not forget that we change too. The more we subject our palates to bold, even shocking flavours, the more we become accustomed to them. Think back to the first time you tried a sour beer, or an intensely bitter IPA. Perhaps this experience may have been challenging, even unpleasant, but now you may find these beers extremely pleasant, from the first sip to the last. The truth is that beer is constantly changing, and sometimes not in the way we expect.

Two of my all-time favourite cask beers are from Peterborough's Oakham Ales, which became the first brewery in the UK to use the North American Citra hop variety when it released the eponymous beer in 2009. But while I love this beer, and drink it whenever I see it, I have an even greater soft spot for its celebrated Jeffery Hudson Bitter, or JHB for short.

'In truth we would now consider Citra and (its stronger sibling) Green Devil IPA to far better represent our identity than JHB,' Oakham's Nick Jones tells me. 'Of course, JHB is a hugely significant beer, not only for starting it all for Oakham Ales but also as a crucially influential staging post in the development of UK craft brewing.'

When former homebrewer John Wood founded the original Oakham Brewery in 1993 he found that the quality of hops available tended to be poorer than today's brewers enjoy using. There was also a shortage of popular English varieties such as Fuggles and East Kent Goldings, and so Paul Corbett of hop merchant Charles Faram suggested to Wood he might consider using North American varieties such as Willamette and Mt Hood. After producing trial batches with both, he chose the latter, worried that the punchy nature of Willamette might be a little too intense for the real ale drinkers of the day. Although, compared to other hops that were available at the time, it was significantly more flavourful and aromatic.

The first batch of JHB was released in September 1993, around the same time as Sean Franklin at Rooster's was changing the game in Yorkshire with his American-style Pale Ale, Yankee. JHB is a little softer than Yankee for me, though, its gentle backbone of malt reminiscent of dry crackers, allowing the floral-yet-pithy lemon and grapefruit nature of its hops to shine bright. The dry finish is almost reminiscent of a good Chardonnay, except at 3.8% it's a beer that demands repeated, voluminous gulps.

It's not the same beer it initially was, though. Far from it, in fact. It's gone through numerous increases in the quantity of hops

John Bryan

it uses, the first coming when Oakham's head brewer, John Bryan, first joined the brewery in 1995. As the brewery has expanded over the years, and the tastes of its customers grew accustomed to more intensely hopped beers, so did the volume of hops in its beers. Today's recipe now uses three times the volume of hops that John Wood used in his initial batch – enough to see it crowned as CAMRA's Champion Beer of Britain in 2001, a feat that its more popular sibling, Citra, has never achieved. Sadly, John Wood passed away in 1998 and never got to fully experience the increasing success and popularity this beer achieved. Thankfully, it's a legacy that John Bryan, Nick Jones and the rest of the team at Oakham dutifully preserve.

'JHB still has a very loyal fan base and remains a key part of our range, although of course it's now a relatively laid back beer alongside some of our contemporary hop monsters,' Jones says. 'It's still a great beer and one that drinkers have been able to trust week in week out for over 27 years now.'

Little Earth Project
Organic Harvest Saison

Location: Edwardstone, Suffolk
Style: Saison | *ABV:* 6.2%

Lambic is a storied beer of Belgian origin brewed in the Senne Valley region to the south of Brussels. Its name is protected under EU Traditional Speciality Guaranteed (TSG) status and production is considerably more laborious and time consuming than other traditional beer styles. It uses a protein-rich grain bill mashed at high temperatures (called a 'turbid mash') plus hops that have been aged between one and five years to create a sticky, sugary brew (called wort, to use its technical name) attractive to yeast and bacteria native to the local atmosphere. These will inoculate said wort as it's left to cool overnight, and the following day it will be transferred to oak barrels where it will ferment and mature for up to three years, sometimes longer.

Typically, Lambics between one and three years of age will be blended and refermented in a bottle to create another style of beer known as Gueuze. This technique creates a spritzy, Champagne-esque beer with voluminous, mousse-like foam and a tart, acidic flavour reminiscent of green apple, lemon zest, and fresh hay. It's remarkably delicious, as is unblended Lambic, if you're ever lucky enough to try some. Although one thing that can be shocking about the latter is that, unusually for a beer, it's almost completely flat, save for the merest hint of micro-carbonation as the native yeasts slowly work their way through any remaining sugar they can find within the beer.

When I first sipped Little Earth Project's remarkable Organic Harvest Saison, released just once a year, such was its similarity to

Lambic that I swear I was lifted from where I stood and transported to the fields of the Belgian Pajottenland. In actual fact, I was under a railway arch at a London beer festival, where the brewery's founder, Tom Norton, had driven down from his Suffolk home to pour his beers. Organic Harvest Saison is not Lambic, in fact, it's made in a slightly different, if not wholly dissimilar way. In terms of its divine flavour, however, this is English Lambic by any other name.

'When we started the brewery we wanted to create beers that were a product of what we could source locally and seasonally,' Norton says. 'This focus on seasonality means producing a variety of beers dependent on the time of year and the conditions that came along with that.'

Organic Harvest Saison is brewed each year in September, using whole cone, freshly harvested hops from the brewery's own certified organic farm three miles from the village of Edwardstone, where they've been officially based since 2015. Norton and his father had been brewing more traditional cask ales for their local pub, The White Horse, since 2008 under the name Mill Green Brewing. Those days are long past, however, with Norton now focusing entirely on wild and mixed-fermentation beers.

After it's brewed, Organic Harvest Saison will spend around five months fermenting in oak barrels, also filled with fresh hops grown on its own farm. While the warmer September weather gives it a chance to ferment, the cooler months allow it to condition slowly, imbuing it with a restrained acidity, and a wonderfully fragrant apple and lemon quality from its hops. Although not spontaneously fermented like Lambic, it is given some assistance thanks to lees (leftover pulp and native yeast) in the barrels, the remains of the naturally fermented cider Norton's father makes in the same vessels.

'The rustic but elongated process that uses barley and hops grown just miles away, water drawn from the chalk below the brewery and local yeast sourced from natural cider make this beer pretty unique,' Norton explains. 'We want to make beer that is natural, perhaps a bit unconventional, but most importantly reflects where we live.'

Burnt Mill
Swimming Giants

Location: Badley, Suffolk
Style: American Double IPA | *ABV*: 8%

Despite being based on a farm in the Suffolk countryside, under the stewardship of head brewer Sophie de Ronde, Burnt Mill makes modern, hop-focused beers that could come from any hyped city-centric brewery between London and San Diego. In the case of Swimming Giants, a hugely intense and aromatic DIPA created in collaboration with New York City's Finback Brewery, that connection is tangible.

This potent brew fuses the sensibilities of both the US and UK east coasts with its remarkably heady combination of Citra, Strata, and Idaho-7 hops from the American North-West, plus the New Zealand Nelson Sauvin variety, which are used to devastating effect. Expect mango, and lots of it, followed by pineapple, lychee, kumquat and maybe even a little lemongrass creeping around its edges. Despite the relative size of its flavour, it is also controlled, elegant even, remarkably masking its high alcohol content with a smooth finish that leaves you wanting more.

Collaboration between small, independently owned breweries is a joy for many reasons, and I can't think of many other industries outside of beer that engage with it in the same enthusiastic manner. On the surface it's a superb platform for knowledge sharing. How many hops go in at this point? What is the grain bill for this particular style? You condition this on toasted coconut and oak chips for how long? Joking aside, the sharing of ideas improves beer quality overall, and is how modern beer styles have proliferated so quickly around the world.

But there's a deeper side to the 'collab', as it is typically referred to. As well as making a beer together, it's about building friendships with like-minded folks from around the entire industry, something that's a unique driving force within modern beer. It's this open attitude towards sharing ideas and forming bonds that has put British beer where it is today, and you can taste this wholesome idealism in every sip of Swimming Giants.

Duration
Bet the Farm

Location: **West Acre, Norfolk**
Style: **Pale Ale**   ABV: **4.5%**

From around 2010 onwards much of the focus and excitement around modern beer in the UK has been in its biggest cities. Take London, for example. At the turn of the century the capital was home to just ten breweries, but – at the time of this book going to print – it is now home to over 140 vibrant and eclectic small businesses producing some of the most exciting beer in the world. It's a story that's as familiar here as it is in places like Bristol, Birmingham, Manchester and Newcastle.

For born-and-bred South Londoner and co-founder of Duration Brewery Miranda Hudson, it would have made sense to lay the foundations of her own brewery in her own backyard. But Hudson has always been the kind of person to buck trends – or start them – and in 2019 she and her husband, head brewer Derek Bates, left the big city behind to start their groundbreaking brewery in the village of West Acre, Norfolk: population 187.

This is no hastily put together, small-scale operation either. Duration is a destination brewery and visitor centre, with a state-of-the-art, German-manufactured brewhouse set into a refurbished, Grade II-listed medieval barn, which allows them to produce beers that are not only deliciously contemporary, but also representative of the rural setting in which they're made. Given that the investment they made in establishing Duration wasn't

insignificant, the appropriately named Bet the Farm is perhaps the best representation of what this brewery does.

'In a literal sense this beer represents us putting our asses on the line with the whole project. There's no real safety net,' Bates, who speaks with the syrupy accent of his native South Carolina, tells me. 'Maybe people will dig what we are doing, maybe they won't but I couldn't die knowing we just did all this work and banged out the same set of beers everyone else seems to and not really push it.'

Inspired by the rustic farmhouse ales of Belgium, Bet the Farm begins life as a resolutely modern take on these classic styles. Utilising Tettnang and Mandarina Bavaria hops to add smooth notes of orange peel and snappy white pepper spice, this is a beer that pairs exceptionally well with an evening sat under a setting sun after a hard day's work. Not all of this beer gets released immediately, however, with some destined for several months of ageing in a large oak vat, more commonly referred to today by the Dutch term, *foeder*. Within this vessel the beer will mingle with both oaken tannins and a multitude of 'wild' yeasts and bacteria, giving the beer further complexity in the form of an almost wine-like acidic bite.

'Duration is about time and place in a beer, reflecting what inspires and informs us from our landscape,' Hudson adds. 'For us, Bet the Farm is an intention to take beer someplace different.'

As a brewery, Duration would be no less compelling to the modern drinker if they had set up in a railway arch in Brixton, or on an industrial estate in Hackney. However, Bates' and Hudson's decision to completely up sticks and do something more dramatic is not merely a representation of their own lofty ambition. As city life becomes less captivating for young creatives and would-be entrepreneurs, theirs is a blueprint for future breweries to come.

Miranda Hudson and Derek Bates

Grain
Slate

Location: Alburgh, Norfolk

Style: Smoked Porter | *ABV:* 6%

Norwich, the self-proclaimed 'Fine City', is a haven for the real ale drinker. From fantastically named pubs such as The Ribs of Beef, to modern beer bars like The Artichoke, and my personal favourite side-street boozer The Plasterers, this is a pub town through and through. When visiting you're never more than a few steps from a fantastically kept pint.

Another excellent Norwich pub is The Plough, which also happens to be owned by Grain Brewery. Based in the village of Alburgh, a stone's throw from the neighbouring county of Suffolk, Grain was established in 2006 after repurposing a small brewing kit that previously belonged to Nottingham's Castle Rock brewery. Its name is a not-so-veiled reference to the fact that East Anglia produces some of the finest barley in the world, including the esteemed Maris Otter variety. Grain has since grown to become one of the most fondly considered breweries in the eastern counties. It acquired The Plough – the first of its three pubs – in 2010, and a couple of years after this it was able to update both brewery and brand identity to one that better reflected the contemporary thinking behind its beers.

'We're what some call an "old new brewery" as we have been around for fifteen years,' founder Phil Halls tells me. 'We came in a little too soon for the craft beer movement, and changing our identity to "craft" runs the heavy risk of being left dad dancing at a wedding.'

I remember well my first visit to The Plough. Around three pubs into a freezing-cold crawl around the city, we bundled in and surrounded the open log fire so as to warm our bones. Perhaps the wintery day influenced my decision, but I fancied a beer on the darker side, and so plumped for a pint of Grain's Smoked Porter, Slate, on cask. The foundation of this beer is locally grown and malted Maris Otter barley, its complexity then increased significantly with additions of amber, brown, chocolate and wheat malt, plus what Halls refers to as ' an expensive dose' of oak smoked barley. For 6% the beer is remarkably smooth, with notes of chocolate, coffee, a little molasses, and at the end just a whiff of sweet smoke, almost reminiscent of maple-cured bacon.

The beer is inspired by a couple of Halls' all-time favourites, namely the Belgian classic, Gouden Carolus, and Good King Henry, a somewhat legendary local Stout that was formerly brewed by Old Chimney's Brewery in the market town of Diss. I say formerly as it is now serendipitously brewed at Grain since its creator, Alan Thomson, went into what Halls describes as semi-retirement. While both Good King Henry and Slate share a similar, delicious complexity, the lower ABV makes the latter a beer to approach repeatedly, and with considerably more enthusiasm.

'I am not claiming to have matched those beers that inspired me,' Halls adds, 'but I am rather pleased with the results.'

BRISTOL AND THE WEST COUNTRY

CHELTENHAM
Deya

Mills   Stroud

Wiper and True
BRISTOL   Left Handed Giant
Lost and Grounded

Yonder
Wild Beer Co

Utopian

EXETER

Harbour

St Austell

Verdant

Think of the South-West of England and you may well think of cider. As indeed you should, for this part of the world purveys some of the most excellent apple-based fermentables. But despite being home to some of the best cider and perry producers you'll find anywhere in the country, the West Country is also home to some of the finest beer makers in the land, from the rolling Cotswolds down to the final stretches of the Cornish coast as it greets the North Atlantic Ocean.

Bristol feels like a great starting point when talking about the West Country, especially in terms of its beer. Here it feels like the creative, libertarian spirit that seems to thrive in this corner of England is condensed into a single vibrant community. Yes, folks are relaxed here, but when it comes to their passions – from art to music to great food and drink – things can quickly get intense. Fret not though, for this spirit is highly contagious, and once you're in it you'll want to throw off the shackles of oppression and head for a pint.

The Bristol beer scene is perhaps best experienced on a busy Friday night along King Street, where you'll find some of the most interesting pubs and bars in town. But as much as native Bristolians take pride in their city and its beer culture, in my experience I've always found them to be endearingly protective of it. Walk into any Bristol pub, bar or retailer with a decent selection of beers and it's the cans and bottles from local favourites such as the Wild Beer Company, Left Handed Giant, and Wiper and True – to name just a handful of its talented breweries – that'll be displayed front and centre. It's exactly the same if you walk into a pub with a wide selection of cask ales, with the majority of pump clips belonging to the city's nearest and dearest. As much as you might be lucky enough to find great beer from other parts of the country on your visit, it feels almost disrespectful to choose something that wasn't made right here in town. This is a city that understands the immense value in that which is small, independent, and local.

This attitude mellows as you venture out into the South-West's expansive countryside, in particular along the coast, where the pace of life is slow, and the joy of a great pint or two is felt deeply. Except, perhaps, in Cornwall, where that sense of West Country pride seems to intensify once again. The beer landscape here is largely dominated by Sharp's (now owned by Canadian giant Molson Coors) and the best-selling cask ale in the country, Doom Bar, along with one of the few larger regional breweries that feature in this book, St Austell. Breweries like these have cemented the beer culture in England's most south-westerly corner with a strong legacy. Conversely, however, it has also provided newcomers with a rule book to tear up – which they have done with little encouragement.

As with much of the rest of the country, peer a little further into the goings on of the beer scene here and you'll find the same fresh, green shoots sprouting. Some of the most exciting brewing talent to have emerged in the past decade has done so in Cornwall, including breweries like Harbour and Verdant. Meanwhile, over the border in neighbouring Devon, those such as Utopian have arrived to shake up the scene with some of the most accomplished beer being made in the country at this moment.

In fact, look anywhere in the West Country and you will find that same inventive, rule-breaking spirit. The beer culture of the South-West is something of a microcosm, encapsulating the spirit of modern British beer in its entirety. Yes, they're protective of it, because they know they're onto a good thing, but demonstrate your curiosity and they'll be happy to welcome you in with open arms, along with a pint or two of outstanding beer.

St Austell
Tribute

Location: St Austell, Cornwall
Style: Amber Ale | *ABV:* 4.2%

To tell the story of modern beer in Cornwall you must first look at one of its oldest and most successful breweries. Founded in 1851, it's one of the oldest businesses in the county that's still operating today, producing millions upon millions of pints annually, many of which are sold via its network of around 170 pubs.

Things weren't always this way though. In fact, the brewery's success only really occurred within the past two decades – almost perfectly chiming with the emergence of the contemporary beer culture we enjoy today. At the turn of the century St Austell was still a relatively small regional brewery, around ten times smaller (in terms of production volume) than it is today. Enter Roger Ryman, a determined young brewer who had earned his master's in brewing and distilling at Heriot-Watt University, before taking a brewing position at Maclay & Co, also in Scotland.

This story has a sad ending, because in May 2020 Ryman died of cancer, aged just fifty-two. But it's an important tale, because it's about how a single, stupendously delicious beer not only changed the fortunes of St Austell brewery but influenced the entire British brewing scene as we know it. Before he passed, I was lucky enough to interview Ryman several times, and he once shared with me the story of how he ended up in Cornwall over a pint of Tribute, the beer that cements the foundation of his great legacy.

In 1999, when he travelled to the opposite end of the country for his interview at St Austell, he arrived the night before and diligently headed to one of its pubs to check out the beer. When asked in the interview the next morning what he thought of it, he told them he didn't think it was very good. The ploy obviously worked, because he was promptly offered the position of head brewer – a role he held for twenty-two years.

That same year was – somewhat auspiciously – marked by a total eclipse of the sun, and to commemorate this occasion, Ryman brewed a special 'one off' beer he called Daylight Robbery. Using Cornish-grown Maris Otter, and a blend of hops – Fuggles from England, Celeia from Slovenia, and Willamette from the United

States – he created a sparkling Amber Ale that resembled the beers locals knew and loved, but with a distinctively more up-to-date flavour. Digestive biscuit and malt loaf provide a gentle layer of sweetness across which notes of orange and lemon zest pirouette into a clean and satisfying finish. It's much less bitter than versions of the style from the North, but retains the fruity, almost floral character from its hops, which make it so satisfying.

The beer was a hit, and soon went from special to a beer that was in constant production. But it needed a better name, and so in 2001 it was launched as Tribute, and is now brewed in 60,000 pint batches at a time. 'Tribute is the catalyst that built the brewery,' Ryman once told me in one of our conversations. 'In fact, the Tribute brand itself has arguably become more important than the brewery, such was the impact it had.'

Ryman would go on to brew other, equally successful and arguably far more modern beers for St Austell, such as Proper Job, its flagship Pale Ale, and the luxuriously decacadent Russian Imperial Stout, Black Square. But it's Tribute that paved the way for the existence of these beers, and it could equally be argued that its success paved the way for the idea of modern beer to properly take root in the South-West.

For me, it's also a representation of the importance of brewing beers that form a legacy. I often look at today's young breweries and try to imagine which of their beers will one day carry the same weight and influence of this beer, and honestly, there are probably very few that ever will. And it's all thanks to one young brewer consciously, and objectively, tasting a local beer and thinking, 'I can do better.'

Verdant
Even Sharks Need Water

Location: Falmouth, Cornwall

Style: New England IPA | *ABV:* 6.5%

It would be nice to say that when Verdant Brewery first sprung upon the scene in 2014 people immediately stood up and took notice. And while in their native Falmouth locals quickly took a shine to their ultra-modern, intensely juicy, and opaquely yellow beers, it took a little longer for the rest of the country to take notice. When they did, however, Verdant rose to become one of the most fawned-over and highly rated breweries in the UK today.

The moment it occurred to me that Verdant is a particularly special brewery occurred, in of all places, Belfast. I remember attending the now sadly retired ABV beer festival in 2016, when a particularly enthusiastic bartender decided my order for me and handed over a glass of Lightbulb, Verdant's flagship Pale Ale. I was immediately captivated by the quality of its pronounced fruit flavours and how well they had adapted the now hugely popular soft and juicy characteristics of the Pale Ales being produced on the East Coast of the US. It's a style the brewery has since made its own, focusing on producing these kinds of beers almost exclusively since its inception. People might say you can have too much of a good thing, but in the case of Verdant IPAs, they're wrong. And one of the best examples of why this is can be found in one of its more regular brews, Even Sharks Need Water.

'When we created the recipe for Sharks we were deep into the haze phase,' Verdant co-founder Adam Robertson tells me. 'We think the beer toes a very balanced line of being humorous and fun, but grown up and well executed. It's soft but sharp, smooth but bitter, fruity but earthy. It set our stall out early doors.'

Sharks uses a potent blend of North American Citra and Australian Galaxy hops to devastatingly delicious effect. But while the latter is now the most cultivated variety in the world, and relatively simple to get hold of, the same cannot be said for Galaxy. While Australia has become incredibly popular for its modern hop varieties, which often take on characteristics, from juicy tropical fruit to herbaceous 'green' and grassy, its yields are far smaller than in the US. This was exacerbated in 2019 when farms were hit with freak hailstorms, balls of ice the size of golf balls destroying almost two thirds of that year's Galaxy harvest in a matter of minutes. Hops are incredibly sensitive to extreme weather, and climate change is something that will have a huge effect on the agriculture of beer if it is not left unchecked. It's one of many reasons why sustainability should be a key part of the modern British brewery's ethos.

Thankfully, the following year's harvest did not suffer the same fate and meant that once again glorious Galaxy found its way into the hands of breweries like Verdant, allowing it in turn to put cans of beers like Even Sharks Need Water into the hands of those who appreciate it. Sharks is classically Verdant, in that while there are potent tropical fruit notes of mango and kiwi fruit, these are joined by stone-fruit characteristics, from apricot to nectarine. Never once dealing in subtleties, the beer is typically bombastic from start to finish, leaving no place for its bold flavour to hide.

Harbour
Antipodean IPA

Location: **Bodmin, Cornwall**
Style: **Australian IPA** | *ABV:* **5.5%**

Situated just south of Bodmin, roughly equidistant from both the Celtic Sea and the English Channel, Harbour is a brewery that enjoys painting the idyll of rural life through its brand. It's something you can practically taste in each of its beers. This is intentional too, as the brewery has quite literally set out a manifesto pledging to produce beers that reflect and accompany their love for the traditional Cornish lifestyle. And when they say this they're talking about hikes along its moors, surfing the waves of its coastlines, and sunsets on its beaches. Perhaps this setting is accompanied by a barbeque packed with locally caught seafood, and definitely a can or two of its bright, eminently refreshing beers that are instilled with a deep and true sense of place.

Harbour's beers are as reflective of their travels and experiences as they are its Cornish homeland. Take Antipodean IPA, for example; hopped with the Australian Vic's Secret and Galaxy varieties, as well as a touch of the German aroma hop, Perle, it's a beer that presents fresh aromatics of passion fruit and lychee. But as colourful as these flavours are, they never appear in a way that's overwhelming. It's a wonderful showcase of modern hop flavour, in a way that's designed to accompany a moment, rather than dominate one.

'When we first rubbed Galaxy hops we fell in love with them,' Harbour's founder, Eddie Lofthouse, tells me. 'We wanted to make an everyday beer with them, not a beer to ponder over or overthink, just something to drink and enjoy.'

When talking about beer being of a certain place, I think it's important to think about its ingredients and how much these are reflective of the feeling that locality conveys. Can a beer be truly 'local' if its hops have been shipped from almost 10,000 miles away? I think the answer is yes, but only if that beer is as reflective of this influence as it is of where it's made – a fine line, which I feel Harbour walks admirably, and of which this beer is a fair representation. In an ideal world we'd only use British hops to convey that feeling, but it's important to remember that the UK only contributes to 2% of global hop yields – not nearly enough to supply even half of the UK breweries if that's all they used. Unless supply chains are to change dramatically, then the globalisation of the hop industry will remain, and so too the myriad flavours that different varieties bring from all corners of the world.

'We're influenced so much by the rest of the world and beer is probably all the better for it,' Lofthouse adds. 'Britain is a wonderful melting pot of cultures and as a society we are definitely better off for it.'

Utopian
Vienna Keller Lager

Location: **Crediton, Devon**
Style: **Vienna Lager** | *ABV:* **4.8%**

In the case of many beers and breweries in this book, I've talked at length about the amazing, diversely flavourful varieties of hops imported from countries like North America, Australia and New Zealand. I do genuinely believe that it's important for breweries to have access to as wide a variety of ingredients as possible (provided there is proper accountability for the sustainability of these ingredients and their use right the way along the supply chain). Modern British beer culture simply wouldn't be where it is now without forward-thinking brewers like John Bryan at Oakham and Kelham Island's Dave Wickett, who pioneered the use of novel ingredients from overseas. Today's breweries deserve the same opportunities.

But now I'm going to flip that idea on its head and talk about something I feel is incredibly progressive in terms of modern brewing. At Devon's Utopian brewing, established in early 2019, they brew beautiful renditions of classic Austrian, German and Czech Lager styles, but they do so with 100% British ingredients.

Can an interpretation of a classic Vienna-style Lager be truly authentic if it doesn't use ingredients of that place? How much does that really matter if that beer is incredibly tasty? This is what I found myself asking when I sipped, nay, gulped down a can of Utopian's Vienna Keller Lager. What makes this particular style stand out from other Lagers is its pronounced malt character, provided by copious amounts of British-grown Vienna and Munich malts, and in this beer this is so well defined in structure it is almost crystalline. This provides ample support for its soft bready notes, and a delicate spicing of hops that ensure every sip is as invigorating as the last. Its cold fermentation and minimum five weeks of lagering time ensures the carbonation is soft and crisp, and never gassy or bloating.

'Our decision to brew with only British grown ingredients came primarily from our sustainability ambitions and a very simple desire to reduce the food miles in the beer,' Utopian founder Richard Archer tells me. 'It was also a pretty easy decision. There are 34 varieties of hops grown in the UK. It's also true that Lagers are often malt forward beers, and we're pretty good at growing and malting barley in the UK.'

As much as I feel it's important to ensure brewers have a wide choice of ingredients to work with when it comes to building flavour in a recipe, it's equally important that breweries invest in those that are native to its own place. In the UK, maltsters such as Crisp, Simpson's and Warminster, along with hop farms like Brook House and Hukin's are, slowly but surely, leading a revolution in high-quality British ingredients. While this doesn't mean your favourite Citra-hopped IPA is going away any time soon, it does mean that forward-thinking breweries like Utopian can indulge in our native cornucopia, and create modern beers that are British in every sense of the word.

Yonder
Boogie

Location: **Wells, Somerset**
Style: **English Bitter** | *ABV:* **3.8%**

When Yonder Brewing appeared on the British brewing scene in 2018 it instantly made a name for itself with its range of beers, from tart and intense Fruited Sours like its flagship Raspberry Gose to more subtle, Saison-style beers in 750ml bottles with clear Belgian influence. But while each of these beers feels quite obviously of the present, Boogie, a take on the classic English Bitter, is the only one of these that feels the need to literally put the word 'modern' on the can.

'Boogie is our nod to the beers which started us on our journey into the world of beer,' Yonder's co-founder, Stuart Winstone, tells me. 'We wanted to combine elements of South West "Bitter" with a traditional Pale Ale, knowing that tastes these days leaned more towards hop flavour, including a refreshing bitterness.'

Even the can that holds Boogie is a nod towards modernity, its purple and yellow splatter reminiscent of a junior Jackson Pollock. The beer itself, however, pours a reassuringly traditional shade of brown, although for the style it's perhaps a touch hazier than usual, with an aroma somewhere between lavender, lemon zest, and a touch of barley sugar. And while this Bitter does indeed have the satisfyingly rounded malt character that typifies the style, it's met by a grassy, citrus-led hop character which gently tugs it – as opposed to dragging it kicking and screaming – into the 21st century. A well-judged dose of bitterness at the end of each sip provides ample encouragement for you to take another swig.

Winstone tells me how Boogie was inspired by trips to the pubs of the South-West, and the same old range of Bitters from traditional, family owned brewers that seemed to forever dominate the hand pulls. 'Here in rural Somerset, and much of the rural South-West, walking into local pubs can be like entering a time capsule,' he tells me. 'Things don't change as quickly here as they would elsewhere.'

In the West Country, Bitters tend to be on the browner and sweeter side, a far cry from the more astringently hoppy and sometimes paler variants which appear in the North. And while there's a nod to this distinctive regionality in its colour, Yonder turned to newer English hop varieties including Endeavour, Bramling Cross, Boadicea and UK-grown Cascade in order to create its more up-to-date flavour. The beer further innovates in its use of Voss Kveik, an isolated strain of yeast originally discovered in the traditional farmhouse breweries of Norway. Kveik ferments far more quickly than traditional English ale yeasts, and while the latter can often impart distinctive flavours in finished beers, Kveik finishes cleanly, allowing hops and malt to shine. It's then wrapped up in a can that is, quite deliberately, designed to stand apart from what we imagine when we think of traditional bitters.

'All of our beers are packaged in cans or bottles with vibrantly coloured labels,' Winstone says. 'We deliberately chose not to make an exception for Boogie because we wanted to bring a younger audience's attention to this beer style.'

The Wild Beer Co
Coolship

Location: Westcombe, Shepton Mallet, Somerset
Style: Wild Ale | *ABV:* 5.9%

The interior of The Wild Beer Company's headquarters in the village of Westcombe, near the Somerset town of Shepton Mallet, is a treasure trove filled with wooden barrels, alongside which stand several *foeders* much taller than you or I. Standing next door to renowned cheesemaker Westcombe Dairy, and just a few miles from the site that holds the legendary Glastonbury music festival, there's a certain peacefulness to the location – a touch of magic in the air, perhaps. Inside the barrel store the air is taut with the musty scent of beer maturing in oak. It's a climate ripe for the practice of the mystical art of spontaneous fermentation and the creation of evocative beers that live up to the 'Wild' element of this brewery's name. One such example is the appropriately named Coolship.

Taken from the Dutch word '*koelschip*', a coolship is a long, shallow, open vessel used to collect wort that will be exposed to the elements overnight. As the protein and sugar-rich liquid cools in the evening air, it's beset upon by millions of wild yeast strains including Brettanomyces (literally translating as British yeast) and bacteria such as Lactobacillus and Pediococcus. Typically done during the winter months to restrict the activity of unwanted micro-fauna, which prefers warmer temperatures, the process is used to inoculate the beer before it's transferred into barrels to undergo fermentation, and several months – or even years – of maturation.

It's a process that stems directly from the Belgian tradition of Lambic brewing (mentioned earlier in this book) now being employed by the likes of the Wild Beer Co to astounding effect.

Once the brewer – in this case the brewery's co-founder, Brett Ellis – is happy with how the barrel-matured beer is tasting, he will pull several batches from different barrels to create one final blend. The art of blending is a part of brewing that is reliant wholly on an individual's sense of taste rather than any technical or scientific method, further adding to the inherently feral nature of beers such as these. Once happy with the final blend, the beer is packaged into 750ml bottles and sealed with wax to stave off the ingress of any unwanted excess oxygen. This allows the beer to be further aged in the eventual owner's cellar, should they somehow resist the temptation to open it immediately.

Andrew Cooper and Brett Ellis

'Andrew [Cooper] and I set up the brewery so we could discover beers like Coolship,' Ellis tells me. 'We apply diligence to stewarding our barrel library for up to four years, but it is when we sit down to taste and blend Coolship that a sense of real discovery and conservancy happens.'

It's a process that in many senses is closer to winemaking than conventional brewing, and not just in procedure but also in flavour. Coolship has a distinctively vinous character, and while not being totally sour, does feature a controlled acidity that carries with it flavours of fig, allspice and orange peel. On the nose there's an almost patchouli-meets-fresh hay character, while the finish is aridly dry, making this beer a perfect pairing with a great deal of different food. Although this may have something to do with its relative proximity to where it's made, I've found an oversized hunk of Westcombe Cheddar to be a perfect match, the tartness of the beer providing the perfect contrast to the silky, fatty nature of the cheese.

Wiper and True
Citra Rye Amber

Location: **Bristol**
Style: **Amber Ale** | *ABV:* **5.1%**

Let's be honest with ourselves for a moment. We give far more of
our time and energy to enjoying pale beers such as Lagers and IPAs
because they're easy to love. There's something almost effortless
in spending time with them, from first sip to that last delicious
swallow. And while we might convince ourselves to turn to the
comforting darkness of Stouts and Porters – especially when it turns
colder outside – as I've previously stated, amber-, red- and brown-
hued beers often get neglected. They are forever the middle child
in modern beer's nuclear family.

Some brewers rightfully turn their backs on Amber Ales
because, frankly, they don't sell. We have to remember that these
are businesses at the end of the day, and they need to keep the lights
on. Thankfully for Amber lovers like myself, there are brewers
like Bristol's Wiper and True, which has not only steadfastly stuck
behind the style since it was established in 2013, but has become
a master of creating many incredibly tasty iterations of it.

'Amber was the first style we commercially brewed and has
stuck with us since,' Martin Saunders, the brewery's commercial
director, tells me. 'A lot of hoppy beers use malt as a canvas, but it's
really fun if you give both ingredients more of a spotlight. That feels
very representative of our whole approach to brewing, aiming to
make beers of our time but with respect for our brewing heritage.'

Inspired by one of the most simple, yet perfect breakfasts – marmalade spread gratuitously across a thickly sliced piece of rye bread – the aptly named Citra Rye Amber merges potent North American Citra hops with both malted rye and barley. Rye is a curious grain, and one I am immensely fond of. Barley is often spoken of as building a 'platform' for hops, but rye is different in that it presents itself in a far more obvious way – a distinctive, golden-syrup sweetness met with a peppercorn crack of spice. It prefers not to hide itself, combining with the Citra to authentically serve you a delicious slice of marmalade-slathered toast, dripping with sweet notes of zesty orange.

Rye also imbues beer with the satisfying amber colour that gives many beers in this style their name. However, its relative popularity compared to Pales means Citra Rye Amber is a yearly, seasonal release rather than being available all the time. I think I prefer it this way, however; beer is a product of agriculture and should forever change with the seasons, from every handful of hops to the last sackful of grain. Thankfully, this is a part of brewing that Wiper and True openly embraces.

'One of the biggest change factors is that the Citra crop varies each year, so the beer will reflect the climate and growing conditions of that harvest,' Saunders tells me. 'But that's in a way we love and embrace. It's part of the beauty of brewing with ever evolving raw ingredients.'

Lost and Grounded
Keller Pils

Location: **Bristol**
Style: **Kellerbier** | *ABV:* 4.8%

A few years ago I was sat with Lost and Grounded brewery's founders, Alex Troncoso and Annie Clements, in Small Bar, a fabulous beer venue situated on Bristol's King Street. Not long after we'd settled, two students arrived at the bar and immediately ordered themselves pints of the brewery's flagship Lager, Keller Pils. Moments after those first satisfying sips, they turned and spotted those responsible for its creation sitting just across from where they were standing, causing them to pause momentarily in silent awe. Nervously, they shuffled over to introduce themselves, and to say thank you for bestowing the city with a modern Lager it could be proud of. Troncoso and Clements were humble and courteous in their response, as they always are, and then we sipped our own pints of Keller Pils, raised our glasses to say cheers, and smiled. It's a memory that's stayed with me; a reminder of how cherished Lost and Grounded are by its local community, and how highly folks think of its beers.

Dry, clean, bitter and tongue-twistingly fresh, with delicate notes of fresh lemon and the peppery, herbaceous snap of German noble hop varieties, Keller Pils, is a Lager that is utterly of the moment. Its name, as with all Kellerbiers, refers to the fact that it is unfiltered and unpasteurised, giving the style its signature, trans-lucently misty appearance. With its version, Lost and Grounded is

BREWERS

Annie Clements and Alex Troncoso

dedicated to preserving the brewing heritage from which it was spawned. It uses only German malt and hops, and even the impressive 25hl brew system that sits at the heart of the brewery itself is manufactured by German fabricator Krones.

However, there's another piece of equipment at Lost and Grounded that is not commonly spotted in British breweries – a lactic acid tank. In fact, when it was installed along with the brewhouse itself in 2015 it may well have been the only one of its kind to exist in the UK. The purpose of the tank is quite simple: it is fed with fresh wort from the brewery and then inoculated with Lactobacillus bacteria, which produces lactic acid as it chomps its way through all that sugar. This acidified wort is then used to 'dose' beers like Keller Pils, lowering their pH, which helps our palates interpret the flavours inherent within the beer, accentuating its hop and malt character, while adding that subtle kick of lemon-fresh acidity.

It's important to note that all beer is naturally acidic (without necessarily being sour). But the lengths that Lost and Grounded go to, not only to preserve traditional German Lager-brewing methods, but also to imbue a character that is essentially unique to what they produce is as refreshing as every last sip of Keller Pils. It gives its beers that intangible sense of place. And while this particular beer is now found all over the UK, it somehow always seems to taste better when enjoyed in Bristol.

'We've always held a core value of being humble and we feel Keller Pils is exactly that,' Troncoso says, 'It's not a beer shouting from the rooftops, or trying to be the next big thing. It's simple, yet extraordinarily complex at the same time.'

Left Handed Giant
Woodland Creatures

Location: **Bristol**
Style: **Milk/Sweet Stout** | *ABV:* **6.9%**

Left Handed Giant has embraced a resolutely progressive attitude since the brewery was established on Bristol's St Philips Industrial Estate in 2015. From its brilliantly vivid can design by resident artist James Yeo, to beers with flavours that scream modernity, it leaves no bases uncovered. The brewery is no stranger to ambition either, and in 2018 opened its second brewery, an impressive brewpub on the banks of the River Avon in the Finzels Reach area, right in the heart of town. With the brewpub focusing on more mainstream styles like Lager and Pale Ale, this freed up the existing brewery to further experiment with alternative flavours.

Developed in collaboration with the Dutch Het Uiltje brewery, Woodland Creatures is a delectable Milk Stout with flavours that come from additions of pistachio and honeycomb, plus the addition of lactose for sweetness and extra body. It leans heavily into the notion that beer can taste like whatever it damn well wants, and that there should be zero boundaries when it comes to experimentation with different flavours.

'I think the combination of big, experimental, impactful beer, alongside bright, vivid, and equally experimental artwork has become something we have definitely become known for,' founder Bruce Gray tells me. 'Woodland Creatures was one of the first for us that really embraced that combination.'

Unsurprisingly, it tastes pretty much like you'd expect, with a rich, syrupy and delicately floral character from the honey, and that savoury-meets-slightly-sweet character that is unique to the pistachio. There's a peculiar level of satisfaction that this beer also provides, which is not unlike draining a bowl of sweetened milk that's absorbed the flavours of a favourite breakfast cereal from one's childhood: except it's almost 7% alcohol. What makes this beer stand out within the so-called Pastry Stout genre, however, is that it's actually pretty accessible. I'd argue even a staunch Stout traditionalist would enjoy this beer, which is something that Gray tells me was completely intentional.

Bruce Gray

'We'd been drinking these huge adjunct Stouts at festivals, and felt like we could create something that was inspired by those beers but retained an element of balance and drinkability,' he says. 'I feel like it was one of the first beers we brewed that really caught the attention of the wider beer public, and helped create a platform and audience for our cans.'

Stroud
Budding Organic Pale

Location: **Stroud, Gloucestershire**
Style: **Pale Ale**   *ABV:* **4.5%**

If there is to be a future for beer in any shape or form, then all brewers must embrace sustainability and make it a central part of their ethos. For Stroud Brewery this has been a core objective since day one. In its own words, the Gloucestershire brewery's mission is to 'make outstanding beer without damaging the planet, and bring people together to inspire positive change.'

In 2018, twelve years after it was first established, it became the first brewery in the UK to become a certified B Corporation. What this recognises is that Stroud is a company that balances its purpose and responsibility to both people and the planet with the profit it makes. Once certification is achieved this gives the recipient the legal responsibility to consider their impact on every aspect of its business, from their customers, to their employees and suppliers, and to the environment. At the time of this book going to print there are now six breweries with the certification, including Small Beer, Toast Ale, Freestar, Brewgooder and, latterly, BrewDog, which was awarded B Corp status in February 2021.

Stroud Brewery, however, is the only brewery on the list to have achieved both B Corp status *and* ensure that all of the ingredients it uses are certified organic. It's the perfect example of what a modern brewery should look like: one that takes responsibility for the ingredients it uses, the beer it makes, and the people who make and drink it. At the heart of this ethos is its flagship Pale Ale, Budding, the first beer it ever brewed.

'When we opened there were far fewer microbreweries and it was still quite a task to persuade local pubs to stock a local beer. To encourage this we decided to champion local characters and events,' Stroud's managing director, Greg Tilley, says, adding that Budding was named after Edward Beard Budding, an engineer of note who invented the lawnmower. It just so happens that the brewery is based in the very same factory where these original machines were once manufactured.

'I could see Pale Ales were gaining popularity and, in tribute to Edwin, I aimed for a grassy bitterness from Fuggles and finished the beer with Amarillo with its fruity and floral aroma,' Tilley continues.

The fusion of English and North American hop varieties is perhaps the most obvious element in this beer to span modern and traditional brewing sensibilities. There's a lovely, refreshing, and indeed, grassy, bitterness, but this is joined by aromas of freshly zested orange peel. This quality doesn't hide the subtly honeysweet structure created by the organic malted barley sourced locally from Warminster Maltings, however, ensuring that this beer is as balanced as the brewery's approach to its people, and its long term impact on the planet.

Mills
Foxbic

Location: Berkeley, Gloucestershire
Style: Beer/Cider Hybrid (Graff)   *ABV:* 6.5%

Every beer that features in this book is undeniably delicious.
The final part of my five-point definition on what constitutes
modern British beer is deliciousness, after all. But there are, on
rare occasions, some beers that exist on another level of flavour
entirely. Beverages that have an almost otherworldly, ethereal
quality to them. Foxbic, from Gloucestershire's Mills Brewing,
is one such example, and also one of the few where I can also say
'I was there' the first ever time it was poured.

Standing among a jovial crowd at the Hereford Beer House
at some point in the spring of 2017, I was eager to taste some of
the finest ciders being made in the world today. Legendary local
producer Tom Oliver had invited his friend, Ryan Burk, of US
cidermaker Angry Orchard, to pour some of his small batch releases.
And while a great many ciders were enjoyed that evening, I was
also introduced to a young, slightly nervous-looking couple by the
name of Jonny and Gen Mills, who were about to open one of their
first ever bottled releases – a beer/cider hybrid they had named
Foxbic. Talk about being in the right place at the right time.

'We were very much inspired by cider maker's approach to
wild fermentation and blending, with an emphasis on minimal
intervention,' Jonny Mills tells me. 'In many ways we are more
closely related to cider producers than the [Belgian] Lambic

producers that originally inspired us, just we use beer ingredients. So Foxbic helped shape our identity right from the beginning.'

Produced in collaboration with Oliver, the beer part of the blend that makes up Foxbic is brewed on a small kit in an outhouse to the rear of the Salutation Inn, a wonderful pub in the Gloucestershire village of Ham. Mills focuses entirely on producing small batch, wild fermented beers, often complex and sour, and on occasion intensely fruited. In the case of this beer, it is blended with juice from a cider apple variety called Foxwhelp, infamous for its sharp and intensely acidic nature. The blend is then fermented in oak barrels on cider lees for seventeen months, before it's packaged into elegant 750ml bottles.

When I took my first sip it was as if the world stopped turning for the briefest of moments. This has happened to me before when tasting certain beers for the first time, but I can count that number on one hand. Before I could even work out what was going on in terms of flavour I knew I had a glass of something incredibly special in my hands, but I eventually managed to wade through its complexities.

There's a candy apple sweetness at first, while aromas of wet hay and lemon peel filter through your nostrils, layers of stewed apples follow next, a little burnt sugar perhaps. And then it hits you; a subtle knife of acidity, creating on your palate the perfect blend of bitter, sharp and sweetness for one fleeting moment. It's so good that you immediately reach for another sip, and then another, and so on. Released just once a year, in batches of less than 1,000 bottles, Foxbic can be difficult to get hold of due to the deserved hype that surrounds Mills today. It's worth heading into the scramble if you can get your hands on a bottle of this magic, however.

Deya
Steady Rolling Man

Location: Cheltenham, Gloucestershire
Style: New England Pale Ale   *ABV*: 5.2%

If someone asked me to pick one beer that, in terms of flavour and appearance at least, signifies modern British beer as a whole, one of the first beers I'd think of would be Steady Rolling Man, the flagship Pale Ale from Cheltenham's Deya Brewing Company.

I've thought about this for a long time, and the reason I feel this beer is so representative of now is how approachable it is. Steady's easy 5.2% ABV speaks to our Britishness and our eternal love of the imperial pint measure. Yes, it's yellow and hazy, and full of juicy, stone fruit flavours reminiscent of peach and apricot, just like a lot of other fussed-over beers that inhabit the New England zone on the IPA spectrum, but here it's dialled in to a point where anyone on either side of beer fandom can enjoy it. If you love intensely hoppy, thick and opaque DIPAs, but fancy slowing down for a moment, then this is the perfect solution. And if you love classic styles but fancy dipping your toe into something more up to date that will delight and not offend? Again, Steady is the answer.

The other quality I love about this beer is how dry and easily sippable it is. The bitterness is just a whisper, which is what makes it accessible to people new to beer, or perhaps even to those who have decided they don't like beer at all.

'Steady Rolling Man [now affectionately known as Steady] was the first recipe we ever brewed. It was a statement of our intent,' the brewery's founder, Theo Freyne, tells me. 'We wanted to make something modern, intense, vibrant and richly hoppy.'

After receiving a master's in brewing and distilling at Heriot-Watt, Fryne then interned for a short while at the esteemed Odell Brewing Company in Fort Collins, Colorado. When he established Deya in 2015, Steady was, for a time, the only beer it brewed, going through what Freyne describes as 'an intense refinement process'. He cites popular modern British Pales such as Beavertown Gamma Ray and pretty much anything by The Kernel as huge influences. But he also speaks highly, and often, of Vermont's Hill Farmstead – widely referred to as one of the greatest breweries in the world – and its house Pale Ale, Edward. In fact, its more sessionable ABV is a deliberate nod to the latter.

Although Deya has since vastly expanded its repertoire of Pale Ales and IPAs, as well as dipping its toe into other styles – from Stouts and Porters to modern takes on Best Bitter – Steady remains the brewery's best seller, accounting for around 40% of production. I've yet to meet anyone who doesn't rhapsodise about this beer after they've tried it, whether they've been drinking beer for several decades or just a few minutes. Now widely loved across the UK, this remains strongest in Deya's hometown of Cheltenham, where locals will gleefully sink pints at the brewery taproom, before picking up a slab of cans to see them through the weekend. At just six years old, this beer is already an icon, and will likely remain so for many years to come.

'Steady is fundamental to us to the extent where it's almost taken on an identity that is as large as the brewery itself,' Freyne adds. 'It gave Deya a platform and an audience, and has been the cornerstone of our business since day one. It's also the beer I'm most proud of.'

LONDON AND THE SOUTH

Anspach & Hobday
Boxcar
Five Points Brewing Company
LONDON ● Queer Brewing
Rock Leopard
The Kernel
Wild Card

Double-Barrelled ●

Ramsgate Brewery ●

Elusive
Siren ●

Good Things ●

SOUTHAMPTON
●
Unity

Beak ● ●
Burning Sky

I will forever be connected to London. Despite no longer living there, it remains dear to me, and I do not yet know when I will stop referring to myself as a 'Londoner'. In Manchester, where I now live, it is immediately obvious to people that I have spent a long time living in the South, from my accent, through to my propensity for forgetting a raincoat when I leave the house.

One thing my fifteen years in the capital did leave me with is an endless love and understanding for its beer culture. I watched as the scene here grew from just ten breweries to one that now encapsulates over 140, and somehow it still feels like there's room for more to join the party. What sets London's breweries apart from those elsewhere in the UK is their determination. Running a brewery is costly in the first place, and it takes a certain amount of grit to keep a small business afloat in the most expensive city in the country, especially when there is so much competition.

For this reason I feel the quality of beer from its younger breweries has not only had to be quickly brought up to a high level, but it has also had to diversify so as to stand out from the ever-growing crowd. Take Croydon's Anspach & Hobday, for example, with its horizontal lagering tanks that help it to accurately recreate traditional German styles, or Boxcar in Bethnal Green, which has taken the traditional English Dark

Mild, and turned it into a modern cult favourite. This is not merely a city of copycat Pale Ales and IPAs, although these styles are also of a bountifully high standard.

Yes, a lot of great beer is made here, but thankfully Londoners have a seemingly unquenchable thirst for it. And with London being such a complex and multicultural city, there's a willingness to embrace new flavours and experiences more openly than you might find elsewhere in the country. This has caused the idea of modern beer to normalise more quickly than it has elsewhere. You no longer need to seek it out, for it is everywhere, from the local pub to the rows of colourful cans stacked in the fridge at your nearest corner shop. For me, this made it the perfect vantage point from which to experience the evolution of modern British beer first hand.

It's easy to forget, though, that there's a great deal more to beer in the South than in the capital alone. While the immensely powerful gravity of London has a tendency to suck people in, especially those visiting from north of the Watford Gap, there are many wonderful beers being produced beyond the reaches of the M25. In fact, you only have to head as far as Reading before you come across progressive breweries such as Double-Barrelled, Siren and Elusive, and experience this to its fullest.

Progress to the south coast and you'll find yet more delights, from creatively minded breweries such as Southampton's Unity Brewing, and Beak in Lewes, to those focused on environmental sustainability, like Good Things, in the hills of the High Weald. Keep heading eastward and eventually you'll reach Kent, the aptly named garden of England. This part of the country is responsible for the majority of the cultivation and stewardship of two of the most important hop varieties in the world today: Fuggles and East Kent Goldings.

While these varieties have had a bad rap over the years (the word 'twiggy' springs to mind) there's a new-found appreciation of these special varieties emerging among today's brewers and drinkers. English hops have a quality to them unlike anything else in the world; earthy, floral, and citrusy. Now, thanks to the

efforts of smaller farmers and the continued investment in
better harvesting and processing technology, these varieties
are once again starting to receive a similar level of admiration
as is bestowed on those that hail from North America, Europe,
Australia, and New Zealand. I'm not arguing that the future
of modern British beer depends entirely on the use of native
ingredients, but I do feel that British brewers should be embracing
them wholeheartedly. As much as great beer is about bold,
interesting flavours, it's not necessarily about accruing air miles.

I understand that for those outside of it, particularly in the
North, embracing the fact that London and the surrounding
southern counties are producing some of the best beer in the
country can be challenging. But, trust me on this one, the beer
is damn good here, and it's well worth taking the time to get
amongst it: whether that's sitting under a railway arch drinking
Hazy IPA in the middle of the big smoke, or somewhere along
the sweeping south coast, enjoying a freshly pulled pint of
English-hopped Bitter.

The Kernel
Export India Porter

Location: Bermondsey, London
Style: Porter | ABV: 6.5%

'I don't think that this beer is the best representation of our brewery,'
The Kernel Brewery's founder, Evin O'Riordain, tells me. 'I don't
think any one beer of ours would. It would miss the point of what
we are trying to do.'

Ever the philosopher, from his trademark ponytail and straggly,
wizard-like beard through to his deeply considered take on beer
and brewing, O'Riordain has quietly presided over one of the most
tumultuous decades in British brewing history. Often imitated
but never bettered, and always quietly going about its business
of making incredibly tasty beer without worrying about fads,
hype or trends, The Kernel is a treasure unique to modern British
beer culture.

'On the other hand, the point of what we are trying to do would
lead to the fact that any one of our beers could equally well represent
us,' he adds, diplomatically.

Without The Kernel, modern British beer simply wouldn't
look the same as it does today. While much bigger and far more
boisterous breweries have emerged from London in the past ten
years, I feel that none have been more influential than it has.
When it was established in Bermondsey in 2009, not far from the
iconic Tower Bridge, there was no other brewery in the country
quite like it. Fast forward to 2021, and there still isn't.

The Kernel's beers have a quality inherent to their flavour that I can only describe as a 'Kernel-ness'. From its vibrantly aromatic Pale Ales and IPAs to their wild and fruited wood-aged beers, right through to their stupendously tasty dark beers, there is not one single dud. This made choosing the beer I wanted to feature in this book immensely difficult. An obvious choice might have been its Table Beer, a low-alcohol, citrus-led delight with near revivifying properties. Perhaps its Citra IPA, a beer that has been cloned extensively by breweries, not just in London but all over the country, and arguably getting the jump on the whole New England IPA craze with its hazy appearance, and showcasing the intense flavour profiles of modern-day hop varieties. I guess 'Bermondsey IPA' doesn't have quite the same ring to it, however.

In the end, I decided to choose the last beer of The Kernel's I enjoyed in their taproom, under the arches at Spa Terminus where they are based today: Export India Porter. For as much as this brewery is admired for its pale beers, its mastery of the dark arts is virtually unparalleled.

After trips to the United States, where he discovered its own burgeoning beer scene, O'Riordain was compelled to take up homebrewing, but opening a commercial brewery of his own was already an ambition. Following the self-published instructions of legendary London homebrewing group the Durden Park Beer Circle, from their book *Old British Beers and How to Make Them*, he began recreating historic Porters. He cites his interest in the style as stemming from a combination of growing up in Ireland (and the ubiquitousness of a certain well-known Stout) and the fact that, despite being the 'birthplace of modern brewing', as he describes it, the appearance of Porter was relatively rare, despite the occasionally spotted Fuller's London Porter.

O'Riordain had a desire to introduce London's drinkers to the wonderfulness of Porter once again. In fact, he tells me that nineteen of The Kernel's first sixty brews were all dark beers. Batch sixty-one would be another, its first attempt at an Export

India Porter. The beer was a hybrid, based on historic recipes from the long-since defunct Barclay Perkins and Amsinck breweries, hailing from 1855 and 1868 respectively, although with his version O'Riordain wanted to bring its flavour up to date by focusing on modern hop varieties.

'With our Export India Porter we decided to update the hopping schedule to imitate that of a modern-day IPA and bring hops and their freshness to the fore,' O'Riordain tells me. 'The base beer without the hops was great, but the additional hopping regime lifts everything and lets it all shine. The hops made everything sing.'

Kernel Porters are typically as unctious as they are aromatic, a thick tan head of foam atop an oubliette-black beer, booming with hop-driven aromas, from citrus and pine to hedgerow and even tropical fruits. Although the hops used change from batch to batch, what typifies Export India Porter for me is a character reminiscent of fresh blackcurrants, with a dank note I find easier to describe as 'green' as any specific flavour. This is all supported by a mammoth amount of molasses, burnt toffee and liquorice provided by the generous use of speciality dark malts. The finish is dry and moreish, and it's here you'll detect that unmistakable 'Kernel-ness' I mentioned earlier. Quite simply, no one else in the country makes dark beers – or indeed any beers – like they do.

'We brew the Export India Porter because it is delicious,' O'Riordain says. 'Porter has always been necessary for us.'

Queer Brewing
Flowers

Location: **Stoke Newington, London**
Style: **Belgian Witbier** | *ABV:* **4%**

When I first met Lily Waite sometime in 2017 I was immediately struck by her mindful approach to beer. Not long after, she would channel this into a career as a beer writer, as well as brewing collaborations with breweries all over the world under the name of The Queer Brewing Project. Her desire, as an openly queer trans woman, was to highlight the lack of LGTBQ+ representation in today's beer culture. In the brief period that followed, she's become one of the most influential figures in modern beer, the narratives she compellingly weaves earning her the accolade of Beer Writer of the Year from the British Guild of Beer Writers in 2020. The following year, her collaborative brewing project would take the leap and become a fully fledged beer business, complete with beers of its own, and its name shortened to Queer Brewing.

While the beers are predominantly brewed in Manchester at Cloudwater, with some now also being produced on an even greater scale at BrewDog in Scotland, Waite –and therefore Queer Brewing – is based at her home in North London. While the majority of breweries that feature among these pages have their own facilities, Waite's project was initially born out of an overwhelming desire to spark change, rather than a more traditional business plan. Thanks to these other breweries stepping up (and notably not taking any profits from the sale of Queer Brewing beer), it's propelled her project forwards at an alarming rate. Queer Brewing's objective is now to secure funding for its own bricks and mortar premises, which – if there's any justice in the world – will be well along the way by the time this book is published.

'I spent a long time imagining just what a Queer Brewing range could look like,' Waite tells me. 'We weren't going to be brewing beer solely for the flavour driven craft beer market, instead trying to reach out beyond the craft bubble and into LGBTQ+ spaces that have been overlooked by craft breweries.'

Flowers is a simple, elegant and, above all, accessible beer, fusing delicate notes of camomile, coriander seed and white pepper with an aroma of dried orange peel. It's the kind of beer that tends to evaporate from the glass when you're not keeping an eye on it. The finish is resoundingly dry, and almost like a white wine, except at a more commensurate level of alcohol. Its inspiration came from one of Waite's all-time favourite beers, Allagash White, a hugely popular Belgian-style Witbier from Maine, in the north-eastern corner of the US.

Before it became known as Flowers, the first ever batch was, aptly, called Statement of Intent. Waite desired to create something that had flavour familiar to craft beer drinkers, but was not off-putting to those outside of it – specifically the LGTBQ+ community that can so often be put off by the inherent white masculinity of beer culture-at-large. For this reason, a Witbier makes perfect sense. As a style it's a little different, but once you get to understand it you realise it's as delicious as any Pale Ale, and as refreshing as any Lager. Culturally, this beer, and indeed Queer Brewing as a whole, is building a bridge that long term will make beer more welcoming, more diverse, and more fun.

'Much jubilation sprung in response to seeing a Witbier included in a core range, including the response from LGBTQ+ folk new to beer enjoying their first example of the style,' Waite says. 'It's been heartening to see our decision to brew a slightly less popular style paying off so far.'

Boxcar
Dark Mild

Location: Bethnal Green, London
Style: English Mild | *ABV:* 3.6%

For many of those who make up the new wave of UK breweries to have emerged over the past ten years, there was a very deliberate intent to break away from more traditional beer styles such as Bitter and Mild. To the latest generation of beer drinkers, these were seen as stagnant, boring and not as interesting or relevant as beers that aimed to pack in the maximum amount of flavour and aroma from the most exciting varieties of hops from around the world. And so they diligently ensured the beers they were producing reflected this.

Over the past couple of years, however, there's been a sea change in the air. A realisation, perhaps, that, done well, traditional styles can be just as delicious and exciting as any explosively hoppy and hazy IPA. This awakening of thought has also been coupled with the acknowledgement that, although sometimes you want to enjoy a beer that holds your attention in the spotlight, at other times you want something that can sit idly in the background, a segue between time well spent with friends. Dark Mild, from Bethnal Green's Boxcar Brew Co, manages to do both with aplomb.

'The idea for making Dark Mild stemmed from a visit to a pub before I was even really into beer, where a Mild festival was happening,' Boxcar's head brewer, Sam Dickison, recalls. 'All the beers were dark, sugary, malt-forward session beers and my memories of that day feel romantic and nostalgic, to say the least.'

Before he brewed his first batch, Dickison took himself to the Great British Beer Festival, where he instigated a personal rule which prevented him from trying anything but Dark Milds. The combination of his own romanticisation of the style, plus the acknowledgement that very few other breweries – particularly in the south-east of England – were brewing them, spurred him towards attempting his own.

Despite Boxcar being predominantly known for ultra-modern and superbly aromatic Pale Ales and IPAs, Dark Mild proved to be an instant hit with its fans. This is perhaps because he had taken a very traditional, yet inherently accessible style, wrapped it in attractive branding, and dispensed via keg rather than cask, a decision that in itself removed a barrier to younger drinkers. It's also because the beer itself is, like all Boxcar beers, incredibly delicious. Sweet, but never too sweet, Dickinson's version of a Dark Mild runs the gamut of brown sugar and golden syrup, the remote chance of this ever becoming cloying ably tempered by a delicate spicing from English hops, adding a drying bitterness to a beer that demands to be supped by the pint.

'I feel we're living through a highly creative and collaborative time for beer,' Dickinson adds. 'Beer as art is a sensory experience, so to be successful is to achieve the experience you wanted. With Dark Mild, I want to give you a memory in liquid form.'

Wild Card
NEIPA

Location: Walthamstow, London
Style: New England IPA   *ABV:* 6.2%

Redolently juicy, with a fruit cocktail of flavours including peach, apricot, melon and pineapple that's typically characteristic of the New England IPA, Wild Card Brewery's take on this zeitgeist of a style represents a huge turning point in the brewery's journey. In fact, head brewer Jaega Wise, who has overseen production at the north-east London-based brewery since it was founded in 2012, describes it to me as 'pivotal'.

'London is such a competitive environment and so we decided to embrace the haze,' Wise says. 'It changed everything for us.'

Before the release of this beer in early 2018, the brewery had largely focused on more traditional beer styles. Beers such as its now decommissioned Golden Ale, King of Hearts, were fermented in open-top vessels just as they still are in some of the larger regional family owned breweries throughout the UK. It also didn't have its own packaging facility on site, and sent beer to a third-party to be bottled, further removing a level of control from the brewery's own hands. With equipment being so expensive and space often being at a premium, this is far from an uncommon strategy for brewery startups. This, combined with struggles to get access to the latest, most interesting hop varieties (Wise explained how she went an entire year being unable to secure even a tiny amount of Citra) meant that the fledgling Wild Card had to do the best it could with the hand it was dealt.

Jaega Wise

As the brewery steadily grew, however, so did its means of production. It was able to switch to modern, closed fermentation vessels, enabling them to extract more aroma from post-fermentation hop additions and produce cleaner tasting beer with more precise hop flavours. Eventually, they were able to afford a canning line and bring all of their processes in house. The first beer to receive this treatment in full was the NEIPA, which both the brewery's staff and its patrons pronounce phonetically as 'nee-pah' in a fashion that feels almost ceremonious.

'It's our most popular special in our range. When it's on the bar, it goes,' Wise tells me. 'Our customers see it as a sure fire bet, and for the brewery it brought with it a completely different change of pace.'

Double-Barrelled
The Big Fruit Heist

Location: **Reading, Berkshire**
Style: **Fruited Sour** | *ABV:* **6%**

Inspired by their travels around the world, during which they experienced and absorbed as much of global beer culture as they possibly could, Mike and Luci Clayton-Jones established Double-Barrelled Brewing in their home town of Reading at the end of 2018. From the taprooms of North America to the *izakaya* of Japan, the beer halls of Bavaria, and more besides, the couple travelled over 85,000 miles in total, before distilling these experiences and allowing them to inform the highly varied and resolutely contemporary beers their brewery produces.

On one particular trip, which led them to the outback of Australia, they came upon a somewhat hyperbolic news headline on an A-board that read 'ALIENS BLAMED FOR MANGO HEIST'. As it happens, Australia is apparently known for what it calls 'big fruit' attractions – quite literally giant sculptures of fruit that people – for reasons beyond my understanding – choose to visit, and get photographed beside. Although this particular 'theft' turned out to be a PR stunt in which no aliens were actually involved, a seed was planted in the minds of the Clayton-Joneses that would spawn an out-of-this world Fruited Sour.

In the early days of Double-Barrelled, the Clayton-Joneses were keen to play around with the acidity and tartness of the historic German Gose and Berliner Weisse styles. In doing so, they found

the salt and coriander present in Gose played well with fruits like raspberry or citrus, but for other kinds of fruit, such as the mango and passion fruit, they didn't initially get the kind of results they desired. In their words, 'a much more in your face method was needed.'

'Having to go hunting in a beer for a specific flavour, especially when the label calls that flavour out was frustrating to us,' Luci Clayton-Jones says. 'From that point on, most of our fruit additions have been fairly sizable, with The Big Fruit Heist being one of the biggest we have done so far.'

Daiquiri lovers rejoice. This beer is a tropical riot of flavour that screams 'serve me by the pool with one of those little cocktail umbrellas.' While it's a universe apart from a traditional Gose, it's not an all-out bomb of fruit sweetness either, with a little tartness creeping in to provide both balance and a mouth-puckering acidity that primes you for another sip. It's a beer that will put a smile on your face, and its inherently fruity nature makes it supremely accessible for those who aren't into more traditional tasting beers.

Siren
Maiden

Location: Finchampstead, Berkshire
Style: Barleywine   *ABV:* 11%

It's rare enough for a Stout or Porter to take home CAMRA's
annual Champion Beer of Britain Award, but in 2018 Siren's
delectable Broken Dream Coffee Stout did just that. Despite
this significant victory, however, when I got in touch with the
brewery's founder, Darron Anley, to ask about including the beer
in this book, to my complete surprise he asked me to include
another beer entirely.

'While I am incredibly romantic about Broken Dream, I feel
that I could write a love story about Maiden and why I would
pick that as the beer that best represents Siren,' Anley says.
'It tells the story of our want to push boundaries and experiment,
and Maiden, like some of our other more experimental beers,
took a while before we really got it where we wanted it to be.'

In fact, Maiden, the Berkshire brewery's annually released
Barleywine, was the first beer it ever brewed after it was founded
in 2013, although it didn't arrive in drinkers' hands until well after
core beers like Broken Dream and Soundwave Pale Ale. Instead, it
spent the best part of a year maturing in oak barrels that formerly
held rum, tequila, madeira, armagnac and bourbon. Once Anley
and his team were happy with how the aged beer was tasting, it was
then time to blend it into a finished product, one that married the
supreme malt-deliciousness of a strong Barleywine with tannins

from the oak, and the ghosts of the spirits the barrels once held, adding a rich, boozy character that warms the back of the throat.

This first release wasn't the end of the Maiden's voyage, however, it was just the beginning. No barrel that ever holds the base beer is ever fully drained, and when a fresh batch is brewed it will be filled on top of whatever an existing barrel still holds. Over the years yet more barrels joined the fold, including those that once held red and white wine, sauternes, port and banyuls. Inspired by Californian craft beer pioneers Firestone Walker, who release a strong, blended, barrel-aged beer once a year in a similar style to mark each anniversary of the brewery, Siren invited collaborators to help decide the individual components of the finished blend. Over the years this has included whisky makers Compass Box, winemaker Le Grappin, and their friends from The Wild Beer Co in Somerset.

What makes each subsequent release of Maiden so special is not only the subtle differences between each release – an extra hit of fruitiness from the tequila barrels, perhaps, or a deep vinous lick of forest fruits from those that held red wine – but also that each year part of the resulting blend will have been in contact with the first ever beer that Siren brewed. It's resolutely a treat beer, one to be sipped and shared with friends once the sun has long since set below the horizon.

'The idea was to create something that would be an interesting conversation piece, a sipper, and hopefully as the years go by something that builds on the heritage of the brewery,' Anley tells me. 'After all, beer is and can be for many a source of conversation, camaraderie and shared experience.'

Elusive
Oregon Trail

Location: **Finchampstead, Berkshire**
Style: **American IPA**   *ABV:* **5.8%**

Deservedly known by many in the industry as 'the nicest man in beer', I first bumped into Elusive Brewing founder Andy Parker in the belly of a London pub sometime in the early 2010s. At the time he was still a homebrewer (albeit one who would win several awards that would lead to him one day owning his own brewery), but what struck me about him was not only how deep his enthusiasm for beer ran, but how infectious it could be – in particular for one of his favourite styles, the American West Coast IPA.

What I find makes the West Coast IPA so spectacular is its ability to showcase hops and malt in their rawest and most undiluted form. I admire and appreciate subtlety in beer, I really do, but I also want it to thrill me, and sometimes that kind of fulfilment can only be provided by intensity. For me this style is about using malted barley to construct a tall, indestructible pillar of caramel sweetness, which is then adorned from plinth to pedestal with the most bitter, resinous and aromatic hops you can find. It might not be the most accessible of beer styles, but it's the one that arguably defined the American craft beer revolution, and was a major catalyst in creating the beer culture we know and love at this moment in time. It's something that Parker has not only hung his hat on, but resolutely made his own.

'My very first home brew was a clone of [San Diego based] Green Flash's West Coast IPA – one of the true classics of the style,' he says. 'In 2019, a customer approached us about brewing a collaboration to help launch their beer club and West Coast IPA was top of their list. I'd been thinking about revisiting that first homebrew recipe and this gave me the perfect excuse.'

Although West Coast IPAs are typically strong and in the 7% ABV region, Parker has put his own stamp on the style by dropping this a little to 5.8%. This plays into our Britishness a little, allowing it to work as well served from a cask as it does via keg. However, during the Coronavirus pandemic, when neither of these options were available due to pubs being forced to shut, Parker decided to can the beer, hoping it would help Elusive reach a wider audience. He describes the response to Oregon Trail as 'fantastic' and in early 2021 it became a core beer, as well as a regular fixture in fridges all over the country.

Amber in colour with an ever-so-off-white head, Oregon Trail drips with the characteristic scent of citrus and pine that this style has become synonymous with. It's also crystal clear, a rare sight in a lot of modern beers, but one I feel is essential to this style, because it needs to finish clean in order to let its inherent bitterness shine. And that's exactly what happens here, while a sturdy malt back-bone leads with sticky toffee notes that prevent it ever veering towards astringency. It's this bittersweet quality that will have you clamouring for another pint the moment you put down the one you just finished.

Unity
Collision

Location: Southampton, Hampshire
Style: New England IPA | *ABV:* 6.2%

By my reckoning, Southampton's Unity Brewing Co should be one of the highest rated and most talked about breweries in the country by now. From the soft, pastel shades of the labels that adorn its branding, to the ochre glow of its hazy beers that are packed with the latest, most exciting hop varieties from around the world, this is as cutting edge a brewery as you like – as comfortable on a bottle shop shelf as it is on an Instagram page.

But for reasons that escape me, its name isn't whispered in the same hushed tones as some of the similar breweries that grace these pages. Breweries like Verdant, Deya, and Cloudwater, for example, who cultivate the lion's share of fuss with their constant stream of limited edition releases. This is perhaps because these breweries have worked hard to develop a feeling of relative scarcity, only releasing certain sought-after beers annually, and stimulating in drinkers the so-called 'fear of missing out' (or FOMO to use its acronym). I don't personally feel there's anything wrong with this approach. There are now over 2,000 breweries in the UK after all, and finding different ways to keep your customers engaged should be applauded. Whenever I return to Unity's superlative IPA, Collision, however, I'm reminded that I can pick up a beer as good as any hyped-to-the-gills release whenever I feel like it. FOMO be damned.

Collision is extrovertly hopped with North American Mosaic and Columbus varieties, imbuing the beer with intense aromatics of ripe mango and orange zest, followed by a dank, bitter note, marrying the best qualities of a modern East and West Coast American IPA. There's another quality in this beer that sets it apart for me, however; a dry, somewhat spicy and almost nutty character it gets from the use of a heritage grain called Spelt, an ancient species of wheat that has been cultivated in Europe since approximately 5000 BC.

'At the time, we were brewing a lot of Saisons with Spelt, which is pretty classic in that style,' Unity's founder and head brewer, Jimmy Hatherley, tells me. 'I had the idea that the slightly nutty and honied notes would work really nicely in an IPA, which turned out it does!'

Despite its mix of influences, Hatherley has taken to referring to this beer as a 'South Coast IPA' in reference to his brewery's home of Southampton. Collision was originally brewed as a one-off for local bar The Rockstone, but when its beer buyer, Bolo Hooper, became a full-time employee at Unity, the beer came with him, and after a few tweaks, became a permanent part of the brewery's range – much to the delight of the beer's sizable fanbase.

'I think our customers really appreciate the fact that Collision is always exciting but also really reliable,' Hatherley says. 'It's hugely representative of our brewery, so it's a favourite amongst our loyal community of drinkers.'

Beak
Lulla

Location: Lewes, Sussex
Style: Table Beer | *ABV:* 3.5%

Lewes is a magical place, set into the gently rolling hills of the
Sussex Downs National Park. At its centre stands Harvey's Brewery,
its iconic tower earning it the nickname 'The Cathedral' among
locals. For lovers of beer, the town is a must visit. Not just because
of the fact that it's home to some of the best pubs in the country,
from the Harvey's-owned Rights of Man to freehouses such as the
Gardeners Arms and the Snowdrop Inn, but because it's also home
to one of the brightest young brewing talents in the UK.

Originally conceived as a 'nomadic' project by founder Danny
Tapper, who brewed itinerantly at the likes of London's Partizan
Brewing and Sussex neighbours Burning Sky, Beak Brewery would
eventually commission its own facility at the start of a tumultuous
2020. In fact, Tapper would sign a ten-year lease on his brewery's
property just two weeks before the entire country was plunged
into lockdown. Fortuitously, a canning line was included in his
business plan, and so, despite not being able to immediately
welcome customers to its planned taproom, it was able to put beer
into the hands of eager drinkers from the off. While some of its
initial offerings such as its house IPA, Parade, and Oopla Imperial
Stout appeal to those seeking beers of a bolder nature, its table
beer, Lulla, is designed for those more interested in nuance and
sessionability.

'These days it can be tempting to create beers that generate high-scoring reviews on [review sites such as] Untappd, namely strong, juicy Pales or massive Imperial Stouts,' Tapper says. 'These styles are great and certainly have their place, but at Beak we like to punctuate them with beers that display a little more balance and finesse – and Lulla is our nod to this.'

Tapper is not shy in his admission that the inspiration for Lulla came from The Kernel's own remarkable Table Beer, which set the modern blueprint for the style, though Beak's version leans further into the New England genre, with a soft water profile and pillowy mouthfeel coming from the addition of oats and wheat. North American Simcoe and Citra hops feature, but instead of intensity bring gentle waves of citrus and watermelon that softly fade into the background. It's the perfect beer to form a bridge between laughter and conversation with friends, which is perhaps why there's no better setting in which to enjoy it than at Beak's own taproom, set against the magnificent chalk-white cliffs of the South Downs.

'At the root of everything we do is a belief that sharing exceptional food and drink with others can be joyful, spirit-raising and maybe even life-affirming,' Tapper says. 'Lulla represents this outlook perfectly as it's a beer that lends itself to being enjoyed in the company of friends, as opposed to being sipped and savoured alone.'

Burning Sky
Saison à la Provision

Location: Firle, Sussex
Style: Saison | *ABV:* 6.5%

Despite being one of the most influential figures in British brewing of the past twenty years, Burning Sky founder Mark Tranter is as quiet and unassuming a personality as they come. Although it must be said he also has an endearingly low tolerance for bullshit. A former art student who enjoyed homebrewing in his spare time, his brewing career began in the basement of Brighton's Evening Star pub, when he began brewing for the then-fledgling Dark Star brewery. He'd work for the Sussex-based brewery for seventeen years, in the early days assisting then-head brewer Rob Jones with the development of popular beers such as Hophead, before eventually becoming head brewer himself, overseeing the brewery's gradual expansion over the course of his tenure.

Although Tranter's time at Dark Star came to its conclusion in 2013, this wasn't an end as such, but the beginning of what has quickly become one of the most special breweries in the country. And while Burning Sky has built a strong reputation for its modern classic cask ales and contemporary IPAs, it's in its comprehensive barrel-ageing and wild fermentation programme where the true heart of its operation lies. The foundation of this is the first Burning Sky beer Tranter ever brewed, Saison à la Provision.

'This was the beer that would help to state our intent with the formation of Burning Sky,' Tranter tells me. 'There was concern in

Mark Tranter

my brain that the popularity of Saison was waning in the UK, but we stuck doggedly to it. I chose to make this beer as I was fanatical about Saisons.'

While visiting the bi-annual Toer de Geuze in Belgium in May 2013, Tranter's long-time friend Eddie Gadd of The Ramsgate Brewery had slung a sack of malt into the boot of his car. This was used to make a 20l batch of beer brewed with another of Tranter's friends and his first employee at Burning Sky, Tom Dobson. Inspired by reading author Phil Markowski's *Farmhouse Ales* the pair decided to experiment by fermenting their beer with three different strains of yeast. Once Tranter had decided on a favourite, another trial batch was brewed, this time with some isolated strains of Brettanomyces and Lactobacillus. Happy with the results, on 30 September 2013 Tranter and Dobson scaled up the recipe to 2,500l, and Burning Sky Brewery was born.

Its name is often unceremoniously shortened to just 'Prov' by Tranter and his small team at the brewery's home in the quaint village of Firle, and before it eventually makes its way into 750ml bottles the beer will spend at least three months maturing in oak *foeders*. This allows the feral yeast and bacteria within plenty of time to slowly chomp its way through the remaining complex sugars, in their wake producing red berry-like fruit esters, plus lactic acid, giving the beer its trademark acidity. While Prov is close to wine in terms of complexity, what makes this beer so special is how approachable it remains despite this. It effortlessly marries an aroma of lavender and fresh hay with notes of lemon zest and manuka honey, buoyed by a little tannin from its time in oak, and an ever-so-delicate effervescence that leads to a finish that is as clean as it is dry. It is without question one of the most accomplished beers being produced in the UK today, and one that's done so with remarkably little ego.

'We had a couple of mantras early on: "to have a clear and unwavering path", and "if you make the beer you want to drink as best you can, others will follow,"' Tranter says. 'This determination to not do things easily, and to have a wild and sometimes chaotic edge amongst our structure is pretty much how daily life at Burning Sky is. I like to think that this beer reflects our passion, quest for refinement, and uniqueness.'

Good Things
Shift in Sight

Location: **Eridge, Sussex**
Style: **German Pilsner** | *ABV:* **5%**

Situated atop the High Weald where the Sussex hills meet the Kentish border, Good Things is a brewery that's as enthusiastic about producing delicious beer as it is about doing so sustainably. It claims to be the first 'closed loop' brewery in the UK, meaning it can run indefinitely without negatively impacting the environment. The brewery's water is sourced from a bore hole that runs 63m below the brewery, while its electricity is provided by a 50kw array of solar panels. The spent grain it uses is dried and milled into flour, which in turn is used by restaurants and bakeries. Soon a reed bed system will be added so that all of its wastewater can be safely returned into the water system and be reused.

While its first year in business saw Good Things largely focus on Pale Ales and IPAs, which can be produced relatively quickly and give a small, young brewery some desperately needed turnover, once they had their feet under the table the brewery decided to turn its focus to Lager. Inspired by traditional German brewing techniques, brewery founder Chris Drummond was determined to get his brewery's first Lager as true to style as possible. Working with a base of the best quality Pilsner malt he could find, plus Mittelfrüh & Spalter Select hops sourced from Germany, soon Drummond, along with childhood friend Russ Wheildon and head brewer Darryl Mills, had a beer in tank ready for its seven-week period of fermentation, maturation and conditioning.

The result was Shift in Sight, a Pilsner-style beer that delivers a crisp, almost herbaceous hit of bitter hops atop a banquet of malt character almost reminiscent of freshly baked bread. The long maturation time, where the beer is essentially stored just above freezing while any remaining yeast naturally produces carbon dioxide, is what gives this beer its classically refreshing character. From a sales perspective, making Lager the long way like this might not be the most cost-effective way of doing so, but it fits perfectly with Good Things' ethos of doing things the right way, regardless of the cost or effort involved.

'As we push on and look to brew beers that are loved by the many it's always great to release a fresh batch of Shift in Sight as it really takes us back to the start of our love of beer,' Drummond tells me. 'We recently went on an IPA rampage, thinking these beers were where it's at. But then another batch of Shift came out and we were instantly reminded why we do what we do.'

*

Sadly, in July 2021 the 17th-century barn that housed Good Things Brewery was struck by lightning and subsequently burned down, damaging the brewery equipment beyond repair. While Good Things had to cease trading as a result of the damage it sustained, it's not the end of the road for this brewery. They plan to relaunch under the name Allkin Brewery in the not too distant future and I'd like to wish them every success in their new venture.

The Ramsgate Brewery
Gadds' Nº 3

Location: **Broadstairs, Kent**
Style: **Pale Ale** | *ABV:* **5%**

If you want to convince someone of the inherent brilliance of
the East Kent Goldings hop variety, buy them a pint (or bottle) of
Gadds' Nº 3 Pale Ale. The trouble is, if you wish to do so then you'll
need to travel down to Kent, because The Ramsgate Brewery, which
produces this ode to one of the finest English hops in existence,
only sells it locally. By doing so it retains a certain level of quality
control. Freshness is paramount to enjoying a hop-focused pale
beer, especially one that's so dedicated to championing a variety
as delicate as the humble Goldings as this is.

'We built the brewery in 2001 with pretty much the sole
intention of making a beer to speak for modern Kent,' brewery
founder Eddie Gadd tells me. 'At the time Sierra Nevada and
[Australia's] Little Creatures Pale Ale were big influences of mine.
Coupled with the local growing of East Kent Goldings, the idea for
the beer took form.'

Pin bright, golden and bursting with the gentle effervescence
that only proper live beer conditioning can present, Gadds' Nº 3
is a wonderful beer – one that somehow gives the impression of
traditional British brewing but then surprises you with a taste
that is resolutely up to date. Despite so often being mislabelled as
'twiggy' or 'earthy' when properly presented in a beer, East Kent
Goldings (EKG) imparts a soft floral character, and a lick of citrus

somewhere between lemon balm and freshly zested citrus. There's just about enough pale malt to hold it all together, but really this one's all about the hops, each glorious sip ending with a triumphantly bitter finish.

The history and significance of East Kent Goldings (EKG) is not nearly as well known as it should be. There's evidence that suggests hop growing has taken place in Kent for almost 500 years, and that this variety in particular seems to thrive here. The warm, dry climate coupled with the cool, saline air drifting in from the English Channel results in yields twice as high as when it's grown elsewhere in the UK, and it's for this reason the EKG has been awarded with Protected Geographic Indicator (PGI) status. Only hops cultivated within county lines can truly be East Kent Goldings, such is the significance of its terroir.

Since he founded the brewery, Eddie Gadd has been sourcing his EKG from Humphrey's Farm on the Isle of Thanet, just down the road from the brewery's home in Ramsgate. However, fans of the beer were dealt a hammer blow in early 2021 when Gadd announced that the farm was shutting down due to shaky forecasts from brewers worrying how the pandemic might affect their beer sales long term. Without a demand for locally grown hops, they will simply cease to be. Thankfully, Gadd has reassured customers that they have enough supply to see them through until at least 2022, meaning that Gadds' № 3 is safe, for now at least.

'East Kent Goldings aren't the easiest hop to use, and they're quite particular, so getting the beer right remains challenging twenty years on,' Gadd says. 'But as local ingredients go it has to rank as one of the best. What an amazing raft to float a brewery on!'

Rock Leopard
How Are You On Your Good Days?

Location: Welling, London
Style: American Double IPA | *ABV:* 8%

Can beer work as a form of protest? Often it is seen as a means of escapism, and as I have stated repeatedly throughout this book, a source of great joy. It's crucial that we hold on to this, but I also believe it's important we shift our expectations in terms of what beer can say, and what it can achieve. Whether we like it or not, beer, like everything else in our lives, is political, and can help shape and even define the modern world we choose to live in.

Following the tragic murder of George Floyd in the US city of Minneapolis on 25 May 2020, protests in the name of the Black Lives Matter movement erupted across the world, including here in Britain. A few days later Rock Leopard founder Stacey Ayeh's day had begun with a much smaller problem; while in the middle of brewing an imperial version of his core IPA, Distant Cousin of a Mu Mu Cat, he realised the hops he'd ordered had not arrived. In between frantic phone calls to the courier trying to locate his missing supplies, his attention turned to social media, and the videos of police brutality filtering through in the wake of the ongoing protests.

Closer to home, he read the story of Sistah Space, a Hackney-based domestic abuse charity for women of African heritage, which was in danger of being evicted from its premises. Dismayed by this, in what he calls an 'instinctive reaction', Ayeh decided to rename the West Coast-style Double IPA he was brewing, calling it 'How Are You On Your Good Days?' Defiantly, instead of waiting for the hops he was waiting on, he used whatever he had to hand, creating a deliciously punchy IPA with flavours of grapefruit, mango and lychee, completed with a delectably resinous and bitter finish. He then donated all profits from its sale to charities, including Sistah Space.

While I maintain the opinion that there has never been a better time to be a beer drinker living on these islands, I also accept that, largely, beer in the UK is not particularly diverse. Of all our 2,000-plus breweries, you can count on the fingers of one hand the ones that are Black-owned. Rock Leopard is one of these, and to ignore Ayeh's beers is to miss out on some seriously good stuff. But if we wish to see modern British beer continue to evolve, then we must proactively ensure that it is open and welcoming to all. By doing so, it means we'll bring a lot more great people like Ayeh, and breweries like Rock Leopard, into the fold.

Stacey Ayeh

Anspach & Hobday
The Rauchbier

Location: Croydon, London
Style: Smoked Lager | *ABV:* 5.6%

'For me, modern British beer is about progress,' Paul Anspach, who founded his brewery with childhood friend John Hobday in 2013, says. 'Over the last couple of years there has been a real uptick in quality. I also think that the sector has matured, with more young brewers embracing traditional styles.' He continues, 'It's all too easy to reject the old in the pursuit of the new and shiny, but we have a fantastic brewing heritage of which we should be proud.'

I remember first visiting Anspach & Hobday brewery under its railway arch in South London late in 2013 on a crawl of what had colloquially become known as 'The Bermondsey Beer Mile'. Not long after The Kernel had established itself in the area back in 2009, other aspirational breweries soon found the affordable real estate being let by Network Rail just as appealing. Soon the likes of Partizan, Brew By Numbers and Anspach & Hobday itself had set up shop with production facilities at the back of their arches, plus makeshift bars and trestle table seating at the front, awaiting the arrival of thirsty punters like myself.

Such was the excitement generated by this sudden availability of beer from the source in the capital that things soon got out of hand. On a Saturday the area became mobbed with excitable drinkers, much to the dismay of some locals, even forcing The Kernel to close its drink-in space for several years while it worked out a more

sensible approach to the madness. In those early days when I first visited, it was relatively serene compared to now, and while I remember Anspach & Hobday beers not being much to write home about, I've since witnessed it develop into one of the finest breweries in London, if not the whole of the UK. In fact, the Bermondsey Beer Mile itself might be the best place to observe first hand exactly how British beer has transformed over the past decade. While it is still very busy at the weekends, it's home to beers of exceptional quality, and these days also has the hospitality to match.

Anspach & Hobday has since relocated its brewery to Croydon, with its existing site in Bermondsey becoming a fully fledged taproom. And while its regular offerings range from Best Bitters to Baltic Porters and everything in between, the beers I most look forward to are an annually released quartet of German-inspired recipes brewed to mark the end of the summer season. Among them is The Rauchbier. Inspired by the smoked beers of Bamberg, it's arguably one of the finest interpretations of the style being made outside of Germany itself.

'I think The Rauchbier is a great case study in our approach to brewing as a whole,' Anspach tells me. 'While it's unique, complex and interesting, it's still balanced. Drinkability and balance are essential to brewing and are qualities that are at the forefront of our minds when we approach any beer.'

Conditioned for several weeks in horizontally stacked tanks specifically designed for this purpose, the beauty of The Rauchbier is that it's a Lager, and is imbued with all the satisfaction and refreshment you'd expect from such a beer. Its use of smoked malt is remarkable; restrained to the edge of intensity without ever becoming overbearing. Notes of sweet beechwood smoke play with the peppery spice of German noble hop varieties, creating a beer that goes beyond a mere tribute to classic versions of the style from Bamberg. The Rauchbier is its own beast entirely, and if this is representative of how beer in London has matured over the past decade, then I can't wait to see what the next ten years brings.

The Five Points Brewing Company Best

Location: Hackney, London
Style: Bitter | *ABV:* 4.1%

Throughout this book I've attempted to showcase what I feel are some of the best examples of modern British beer. At one point I stated that a beer like Deya Brewing Co's Steady Rolling Man – a hazy, juicy Pale Ale using the most cutting-edge ingredients and brewing techniques available – epitomises how far beer in the UK has come over the past twenty or thirty years. And while this is a beverage that represents both deliciousness and accessibility for drinkers new and old, I'm now going to contradict myself.

Putting this book together has been as much of a journey of learning and discovery for me as it no doubt has been for you. Although I am a purveyor of strong opinions, I find it wise to hold them loosely. And after taking the time to work out exactly what modern British beer is, I think I've finally figured out the kind of beer that best represents our country's beer culture: the most modern, most out there, most progressive beer being brewed in the UK today is a Best Bitter, brewed with Fuggles and Maris Otter.

Hear me out for a moment. Advancements in British brewing culture have typically come from those with a desire to force change, whether purposely or accidentally. When CAMRA was founded in 1971 it was with the direct intention to campaign against the objectives of mass-produced national beer brands which they saw as destroying the culture they loved. When the likes of Sean Franklin

and Dave Wickett saw the potential in bold, new North American hop varieties, despite the fact that their flavour would be off putting to many, they pushed on, because they knew people would get it eventually. Through their tenacity they gradually overcame the preconceptions and boundaries that prevented people from enjoying a host of new flavours. Now hops like these are the most widely cultivated and popular in the world.

Then came BrewDog, which decided to rage against the institution of British beer, from its traditional real ale culture and family brewer history, right through to the best-selling, mass-produced Lagers that still dominate the market even today. Eventually, it would grow so large it would become part of the very system it opposed, but not before it injected a much-needed dose of attitude, modernising beer's outlook and opening up its culture to a great many more people as it grew. But the true essence of modern British beer isn't in the breweries that are loud, brash and in your face. It's in the breweries you might never have heard of, working hard in the background, making the best beer they possibly can. The Marbles, The Kernels and the Burning Skys. Those who are respectful of brewing heritage and tradition, but always working to produce something delicious, satisfying and joyful.

Five Points Best represents this way of thinking, distilled into a perfect moment, in the shape of a pint of cask beer. A majestic fusion of English ingredients, including Fuggles acquired from dedicated hop farmer Hukin's in Kent, with whom the brewery works directly to ensure they are of the utmost quality. Their lemony, peppery snap works in perfect harmony with the delicate sweetness of Maris Otter malted barley; its amber colour enticing, its brightness and clarity a mark of care and quality, its dry, subtly spicy finish designed to make you think about your second pint, or even your third, before you're even halfway through your first.

'Cask beer has clearly had a rough ride over the last few years, but I think with a commitment to quality it will endure,' Greg Hobbs, Five Points' co-founder and head brewer tells me. 'Well-made and properly cared for cask beer is the epitome of modern British beer.'

Hobbs is correct. Sure, American-style IPAs are delicious. So are Belgian-inspired Saisons and sweetened-to-the-eyeballs Pastry Stouts. But you can't find a perfect pint of cask bitter anywhere else in the world other than right here in the UK. It is uniquely our own, and when done with great care and the best ingredients and processes available to the brewer, there is nothing that could be more perfect, and indeed, more modern in terms of British beer.

But, as we've hopefully learned, delicious beer alone does not make for modernity. To be truly modern, beer must also speak of its place, and to its community – including those who are underserved and underrepresented by it. It must be respectful of its agriculture and environmentally sustainable so that it can be enjoyed as much by this generation as it should the next, and the one after that. Yes, we drink beer because it brings us joy, but with that enjoyment also comes a certain amount of responsibility. Beer is a great leveller, and should be for everyone, but we must accept that it isn't always. Only when beer is truly open and accessible to all, then, and only then, can it genuinely be called modern.

And when it is, I'll drink to that.

Further Reading

Right at the start of *Modern British Beer* I made it clear that this wasn't a history book, or a guide to beer. If, after reading it, you want to know more about the world's greatest beverage, then there are plenty of excellent reads out there to enhance your beer knowledge. Here are a few of my favourites to get you started.

BERNSTEIN, Joshua M., *The Complete Beer Course* (Sterling Press, 2013)

BOAK, Jessica, and BAILEY, Ray, *Brew Britannia* (Aurum Press, 2017)

BROWN, Pete, *Man Walks into a Pub* (Pan, 2nd edn, 2010)

BROWN, Pete, *Miracle Brew* (Unbound, 2018)

BULLEN, Claire, and FERGUSON, Jen, *The Beer Lover's Table* (Dog & Bone, 2019)

COLE, Melissa, *The Little Book of Craft Beer* (Hardie Grant, 2017)

CORNELL, Martyn, *Amber, Gold and Black* (History Press, 2010)

DREDGE, Mark, *A Brief History of Lager* (Kyle Books, 2019)

MOSHER, Randy, *Tasting Beer* (Storey Publishing, 2nd edn, 2017)

OLIVER, Garrett, *The Oxford Companion to Beer* (OUP USA, 2011)

PROTZ, Roger, *The Family Brewers of Britain* (CAMRA Books, 2020)

TIERNEY-JONES, Adrian, *The Seven Moods of Craft Beer* (8 Books, 2017)

TIERNEY-JONES, Adrian, and PROTZ, Roger, *Britain's Beer Revolution* (CAMRA Books, 2014)

WATSON, Natalya, *Beer: Taste the Evolution in 50 Styles* (Kyle Books, 2020)

WEBB, Tim, and BEAUMONT, Stephen, *The World Atlas of Beer* (Mitchell Beazley, 2020)

PHOTO CREDITS

With thanks to all the breweries and individuals who supplied images for use in this book.

Matthew Curtis p. 7, 8–9, 13, 15, 19, 21, 22-23, 28, 30, 32, 34, 43, 45, 51, 54, 73, 79, 90, 93, 105, 107, 117, 120, 121, 128, 143, 150, 153, 155, 175, 181, 183, 187, 201, 202, 211, 217, 218, 224–5, 226, 229, 231, 232, 234, 246, 248, 257, 259, 264, 271, 272, 280, 283, 285; Sam Harris p. 268; Ute Kanngiesser p. 249; Lily Waite p. 250.

CAMRA Books

Modern British Cider
GABE COOK

Cider is one of the world's oldest drinks, with a heritage dating back at least 2,000 years. It formed an integral part of the landscape, economy and culture of many rural parts of the UK for centuries before being commoditised by industrial-scale production. Cider now faces a new change in the drinking landscape of Britain — the rise of craft drinks, which brings with it modern, discerning drinkers with different needs, habits and spending opportunities. Acclaimed cider expert Gabe Cook celebrates the heritage, diversity and innovation within the wonderful world of British cider today.

RRP **£15.99** ISBN 978-1-85249-371-4

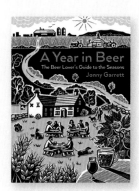

A Year in Beer
JONNY GARRETT

Chefs have been telling us to eat seasonally for decades, yet, when it comes to drink, we tend to reach for the same thing, whatever time of year. But beer is inextricably linked to the seasons, and thinking about it all seasonally opens the door to even greater beer experiences. *A Year in Beer* is an exploration of how our ingredients and tastes change with the seasons, and how Britain's rich brewing history still influences us today. Discover the best UK beer experiences, from summer beer festivals to the autumn hop and apple harvests — taking in the glory of the seasons that make them all possible.

RRP **£15.99** ISBN 978-1-85249-372-1

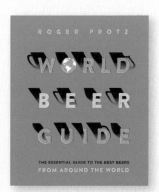

World Beer Guide
ROGER PROTZ

The world of beer is on fire. Traditional brewing countries are witnessing a spectacular growth in the number of beer makers while drinkers in such unlikely nations as France and Italy are moving from the grape to the grain. Drawing on decades of experience, Roger Protz takes readers on a journey of discovery around the world's favourite alcoholic drink — uncovering the interlinked stories behind the best breweries and beers across every continent in the world.

RRP **£30** ISBN 978-1-85249-373-8

Order these and other CAMRA Books from **shop.camra.org.uk**

*Thank you to all of the
following who pledged support
for this publication*

D. CAREW

ANDY GRAYDON

JOYLON GRIFFITHS

STUART HASSAL

PHILIP G. MASON

GEORGE IRVIN OLD

DARRELL JOHN POTENTE

FRANK O'REILLY